TALKING TO GIRLS ABOUT DURAN DURAN

ROB SHEFFIELD is a columnist for *Rolling Stone,* where he writes about music, TV, and pop culture. He regularly appears on VH1, and is the author of the national bestseller *Love Is a Mix Tape: Life and Loss, One Song at a Time.* He lives with his wife in Brooklyn.

Praise for *Talking to Girls About Duran Duran*

"A winning memoir." —*Austin American-Statesman*

"Heartfelt and penetrating . . . sparkling writing." —*Los Angeles Times*

"Rob Sheffield's essays on some of the era's most egregious songs are a hilarious memoir of growing up shy, Catholic, and a huge Hall & Oates fan in the decade that taste forgot." —*Time*

"[Sheffield]'s such a funny and insightful critic . . . After happily wallowing in this nostalgic journey, haul out your Go-Go's tunes, and you'll soon feel the same." —*The Miami Herald*

"Packed with the same subtle wit, charm, and encyclopedic knowledge of '80s music that made him such an endearing and sympathetic narrator the first time around." —*The Boston Globe*

"A touchingly funny memoir of Sheffield's teenage years." —*Family Circle*

"A lighthearted coming-of-age story about a music-addicted teen growing up in '80s Boston, driving an ice cream truck and gobbling up all things new wave. We all have songs that serve as emotional and biographical touchstones, but Sheffield has a gift for writing about such songs and bands in a way that brings his past to vivid life." —*The Dallas Morning News*

"Sheffield's fellow early MTV worshippers [will be] happy to connect with such a delightfully wistful, new-wave kindred spirit." —*The Washington Post*

Praise for *Love Is a Mix Tape*

"A memoir that manages—no small feat—to be funny and beautifully forlorn at the same time."   —*The New York Times Book Review*

"Humorous, heartbreaking, and heroic."   —*Entertainment Weekly*

"Sheffield writes elegantly without turning it into a depressing tale of love stolen away too soon. . . . Wry and sardonic, even in his suffering, he's the tragic romantic who never gets overwrought."   —*Newsweek*

"The finest lines ever written about rock'n'roll . . . Like that song on the radio, every word of Rob's book is true. Love is a mix tape."   —*Rolling Stone*

"Many of us use pop culture as a mirror of our emotional lives, but Sheffield happily walks right through the looking glass."   —*Los Angeles Times*

"This is a lightly handed, skillful, and sincere celebration of pop, of love, sad songs, bad songs, and the long, nearly unbearable ache of being a young widower. Witty and wise; a true candidate for the All-Time Desert Island Top 5 Books About Pop Music."   —*Kirkus Reviews* (starred)

"I can't think of many books as appealing as Rob Sheffield's *Love Is a Mix Tape*; Sheffield writes beautifully about music; he's hilarious; and his story is alternatingly joyous and heartbreaking. Plus, everyone knows there's no better way to organize history and make sense of life than through the mix tape."
                    —Haven Kimmel, bestselling author of *She Got Up Off the Couch*,
                         A Girl Named Zippy, and *The Solace of Leaving Early*

"A celebratory eulogy of life 'in the decade of Nirvana.'"
                                          —*Publishers Weekly* (starred review)

"Sheffield's description of Renée's brilliant eccentricity and lovable quirkiness causes the reader to fall in love with her just as he does."
                                          —*Library Journal* (starred review)

"A glorious elegy to a pop-culture-blessed decade and a tender, unforgettable tribute to the power of love."   —*The Miami Herald*

ALSO BY ROB SHEFFIELD:

LOVE IS A MIX TAPE: LIFE AND
LOSS, ONE SONG AT A TIME

talking to girls about duran duran

ONE YOUNG MAN'S QUEST FOR TRUE LOVE AND A COOLER HAIRCUT

ROB SHEFFIELD

A PLUME BOOK

PLUME
Published by Penguin Group (USA) Inc.
375 Hudson Street, New York, New York 10014, U.S.A. • Penguin Group (Canada), 90 Eglinton Avenue East, Suite 700, Toronto, Ontario, Canada M4P 2Y3 (a division of Pearson Penguin Canada Inc.) • Penguin Books Ltd., 80 Strand, London WC2R 0RL, England • Penguin Ireland, 25 St. Stephen's Green, Dublin 2, Ireland (a division of Penguin Books Ltd.) • Penguin Group (Australia), 250 Camberwell Road, Camberwell, Victoria 3124, Australia (a division of Pearson Australia Group Pty. Ltd.) • Penguin Books India Pvt. Ltd., 11 Community Centre, Panchsheel Park, New Delhi – 110 017, India; Penguin Group (NZ), 67 Apollo Drive, Rosedale, North Shore 0632, New Zealand (a division of Pearson New Zealand Ltd.) • Penguin Books (South Africa) (Pty.) Ltd., 24 Sturdee Avenue, Rosebank, Johannesburg 2196, South Africa

Penguin Books Ltd., Registered Offices: 80 Strand, London WC2R 0RL, England

Published by Plume, a member of Penguin Group (USA) Inc.
Previously published in a Dutton edition.

First Plume Printing, May 2011
1 3 5 7 9 10 8 6 4 2

Ⓟ REGISTERED TRADEMARK—MARCA REGISTRADA

The Library of Congress has catalogued the Dutton edition as follows:

Sheffield, Rob.
Talking to girls about Duran Duran : one young man's quest for true love
and a cooler haircut / Rob Sheffield.—1st ed.
p. cm.
ISBN 978-0-525-95156-8 (hc.)
ISBN 978-0-452-29723-4 (pbk.)
1. Sheffield, Rob. 2. Music critics—United States—Biography. 3. Journalists—
United States—Biography. 4. Rock music—History and criticism. I. Title.
ML423.S537A3 2010
781.64092—dc22
[B]   2010018636

Printed in the United States of America
Original hardcover design by Maria Elias

Penguin is committed to publishing works of quality and integrity.
In that spirit, we are proud to offer this book to our readers;
however, the story, the experiences, and the words
are the author's alone.

for Ally

Contents

CONTENTS

CONTENTS

"LOOK AT THE TWO PEOPLE DANCING ON EITHER
SIDE OF YOU. IF YOU DON'T SEE A GIRL,
YOU ARE DANCING INCORRECTLY."

—THE KEYBOARDIST FOR LCD SOUNDSYSTEM

If you ever step into the Wayback Machine and zip to the 1980s, you will have some interesting conversations, even though nobody will believe a word you say. You can tell people the twentieth century will end without a nuclear war. The Soviet Union will dissolve, the Berlin Wall will come down, and people will start using these things called "ringtones" that make their pants randomly sing "Eye of the Tiger." America will elect a black president who spent his college days listening to the B-52s.

But there's one claim nobody will believe: Duran Duran are still famous.

I can't believe it myself. I've always been a Duran Duran fan. I was an '80s kid, so I grew up on them. I watched Simon Le Bon and Nick Rhodes give "Save a Prayer" its world premiere live on MTV. I listened hard to the lyrics of "Is There Something I Should Know?" and pondered its existential vision of romantic love. I have studied their fashion, learned their wives' names, bought their solo albums. I've always been obsessed with Duran Duran. But even more so, I've been obsessed with how girls talk about them. I'm pretty sure Duran Duran would cease to exist if girls ever stopped talking about them. Except they never do.

Talking to girls about Duran Duran? It's how I've spent my

life. I count on the Fab Five to help me understand all the females in my life—all the crushes and true loves, the sisters and house-mates, the friends and confidantes and allies and heroes. Girls like to talk, and if you are a boy and you want to learn how to listen to girl talk, start a conversation and keep it going, that means you have to deal with Duran Duran. You learn to talk about what the girls want to talk about. And it is a truth universally acknowledged that the girls want to talk about Duran Duran.

My little sister Caroline understands. "It's like talking to boys about wrestling," she says. "You can't just name check, oh, Hulk Hogan or Roddy Piper, because all that means is you used to watch WWF with your brother. So you have to act casual and mention Billy Jack Haynes or Hercules Hernandez. Then the boys are putty in your hands."

I've never heard of these wrestlers, though I assume my sister knows what she's talking about. But I guess Duran Duran are an obsession for me because they were the girls' band that I loved and because I loved them at a time when I was figuring out what it meant to be a guy. So trying to figure them out is how I keep figuring myself out.

There's a character in a Kingsley Amis novel who asks, "Why did I like women's breasts so much? I was clear on why I liked them, thanks, but why did I like them *so much*?" I wonder the same thing about Duran Duran. I get why women love them, but why do women love them *so much*? I feel like if I could solve that riddle, I could solve a lot of others.

•   •   •

The Durannies liked girls. Like Bowie or the Beatles, they liked girls enough to want to look like girls. The admiration was mutual, and at this point they have been famous and beloved for thirty years. It's fair to say that at the time, we all thought this band would be forgotten by now, yet everyone in the Western world can still sing "Hungry Like the Wolf." Simon, Nick, John, Andy and Roger remain icons of adolescent female desire. Even the tenderoni who weren't even born in the '80s know what "Girls on Film" is about and nurture that special relationship all ladies seem to share with John. (Sometimes also Roger. Frequently Simon. Not Andy.) How did this happen?

The '80s, obviously. I was thirteen when the '80s began and twenty-three when they ended, so this was the era of my adolescence, and I never figured anybody would remember the '80s fondly after they were over. But like everything else that happened in the '80s, Duran Duran symbolize teenage yearnings. Girls still grow up memorizing *Pretty in Pink* and *Dirty Dancing* during those constant weekend TV marathons. Any time *Sixteen Candles* comes on, my sisters can recite every scene word for word. (If I'm lucky, I get in a few Jake lines.) When Michael Jackson, John Hughes and Patrick Swayze died, these were national days of mourning. Every night in your town, you can find a bar somewhere hosting an Awesome '80s Prom Night, where you can count on a steady loop of "Tainted Love" and "Billie Jean" and "Just Like Heaven." Any wedding I attend degenerates into a room full of Tommys and Ginas screaming "Livin' on a Prayer." If that *doesn't* happen, the couple could probably get an annulment.

If you were famous in the '80s, you will never be *not* famous. (In theoretical physics, this principle is formally known as the Justine Bateman Constant.) Any group that was popular in the '80s can still pack a room. When '80s darlings Depeche Mode come to town, my wife, Ally, begins picking out her dress weeks before the show, even though I already know it's going to be the short black one. And I know I'm her date for the show, and I know she will look deep into my eyes when Dave Gahan sings "A Question of Time." We played Kajagoogoo's "Too Shy" at our wedding and nobody even walked out.

I've built my whole life around loving music. I'm a writer for *Rolling Stone*, so I am constantly searching for new bands and soaking up new sounds. When I started out as a music journalist, at the end of the 1980s, it was generally assumed that we were living through the lamest music era the world would ever see. But those were also the years when hip-hop exploded, beatbox disco soared, indie rock took off, and new wave invented a language of teen angst. All sorts of futuristic electronic music machines offered obnoxious noises for the plundering. All kinds of bold feminist ideas were inspiring pop stars to play around with gender roles and sexual politics, on a level that would have been unthinkable just a few years earlier. The radio could be your jam, whether you were a new-wave kid, a punk rocker, a disco fan, a hip-hop head, a Morrissey acolyte or a card-carrying member of the Cinderella Fan Club. I was every one of these at some time or another—I loved it all.

But even I didn't think there was so much going on in the

'80s that people would still be trying to figure out all these years later. I didn't expect I'd still be trying to figure it out either. A few years ago, I went to the Rocklahoma festival, devoted to the '80s hair-metal bands. I stood in a field, surrounded for the first and last time by thirty thousand of my fellow Quiet Riot fans, listening to the band play "Metal Health (Bang Your Head)." Was it strange? Very. Did it rock? Brutally.

It's always weird to see how the Hair Decade lives on, even for people barely old enough to remember it. Every week, in my neighborhood of Greenpoint, Brooklyn, I go and see young bands getting brand-new kicks out of '80s beats. At the time, we all figured we were stuck in an Epoch of Bogus. The country was in horrific shape, with Reagan and his cronies running amok. It was customary to blame music for the poisonous state of the nation. Nobody would have suspected that anyone would ever go to the movies to relive 1985 (*The Wedding Singer*), 1987 (*Adventureland*) or, Jesus, 1986 (*Hot Tub Time Machine*). I mean, the biggest movie of 1985 was the one where Michael J. Fox used a time machine to get the hell *out* of 1985. We were young, bored and dumb, so we couldn't wait for it all to end. But something has kept this all alive. And in retrospect, the Epoch of Bogus evolved into the Apex of Awesome. Who made this decision?

Girls, obviously. As Tone Loc said, "This is the Eighties and I'm down with the ladies." The ladies were not necessarily down with Tone Loc—but they're down with the '80s, and it's feminine passion that sustains the whole mythology of '80s teen dreams. And of all the absurd and perverted artifacts from that time, nothing keeps them feeling fascination like Duran Duran. Which is why I've always been fascinated too. How the hell did men and women communicate before they had this band to discuss? Fortunately, I'll never have to know.

The first girls I shared them with were my high school pals Heather and Lisa, girlie girls who liked to talk about Duran Duran because they liked to say the name, which they pronounced, "Jran Jran." Heather and Lisa taught me about sushi, high heels, "Wake Me Up Before You Go-Go," the value of earrings shaped like pieces of sushi, and the importance of never letting Lisa drive your car—but the most crucial lesson was Duran Duran. We would go out for ice cream and they would sing along with the radio, using spoons for mikes, and we would wait until the next time "Union of the Snake" or "Hungry Like the Wolf" came on WHTT, which was never a long wait.

Lisa's cousin was a model who was married to the keyboardist in this band, and she went to their wedding. We grilled her for the details—apparently her uncle gave a moving toast, which was drowned out by the ecstatic squeals of Roger Taylor's date in the backless dress as he licked her entire spine, vertebra by vertebra. Lisa also had sordid backstage gossip of drugs and sex. But what really mattered to me? The way Lisa said their name: "Jran Jran." I tried to say it that way too.

Heather and Lisa had disposable boyfriends who suffered at their hands and made me secretly feel grateful to be above such things. I was better at being a girlfriend than a boyfriend anyway. I wasn't really living the Duran Duran lifestyle, which seemed to involve dedicating your life to traveling to distant locales where you would flip over tables and pour champagne for pouty vixens who would help you apply your mascara. I might have been a shy, bookish geek, but I was totally hung up on this pop group who were devoted to sex and glamour and danger. I loved how fiercely girls loved DD, and how fearless DD were in the face of so much girl worship. I was pretty sure I had a lot to learn from these guys.

I envied the religious intensity of their fandom. One day, you're a perfectly ordinary suburban princess, content with Journey and Styx, and then you hear something new and all of a sudden you're one of *those girls*. It's funny because a female audience is often a fickle audience, and yet it goes both ways. A "girls' artist," whether it's Depeche Mode or Neil Diamond or Duran Duran or Jeff Buckley or Luther Vandross or R.E.M. or the New Kids, commands a certain loyalty that never really goes away. An adult woman might have a slightly mocking, slightly ironic relationship to her teenage Duran-loving self, and yet she can still feel that love in a non-ironic way. And when adult women talk about them, they turn into *those girls* again.

That's why Duran Duran always keep coming up in conversation, no matter where I am or who I'm talking to. A few weeks ago, I went to see a band called the Cribs at the Bowery Ballroom in New York and wound up at the bar talking to a music-industry lawyer who represents the biggest names in hip-hop. Within five minutes, she was raving about John Taylor. She'd just been in the Bahamas, staying at a posh resort where (by coincidence) Duran

Duran were staying, in rehearsals for their upcoming reunion tour. She was in the pool with John Taylor, swimming past him in her bikini, trying to turn his head, telling herself, "I am swimming in John Taylor's water. The chlorine touching his body is touching mine."

This woman obviously loves them in a way that's very different from how I love them, yet in some ways not so different, and I guess those differences intrigue me. Even if I didn't share those dreams of splashing in John Taylor's backwash, I definitely associated the music with sexual yearning, and I loved how girls would get a certain glow in the throes of pop passion. My feelings for these girls could get all mixed up in identification with the band—maybe girls would scream for me the way they screamed for DD if only I modeled my life on Simon Le Bon, and borrowed his lipliner, and spiced my conversation with lines like "My mouth is alive with juices like wine." It might take years of monastic devotion. I might have to go to exotic locales and have sex with actual wolves.

When I had my first actual girlfriend, she tried putting makeup on me; I begged her to "give me the Nick Rhodes," although I was secretly hoping she would accidentally give me the John Taylor. As a die-hard punk rock chick, she hated Duran Duran, but she liked the idea of a boyfriend who looked a little bit more like John Taylor. Unfortunately, I ended up looking kind of like Andy Taylor's bag-lady auntie. I had to face the facts. Being Duran Duran was never going to be an option. I would have to settle for being a fan.

When you're a boy, you sometimes begrudge the rock stars

who are bogarting your share of feminine attention. When I met Peter Buck of R.E.M., he mentioned something I'd written about resenting how much girls loved his band. I was mortified, but he just smiled and said, "In my day, it was David Bowie. I was mad at him because my girlfriends liked him better than me."

Duran Duran rank high on this chart. Boys always hated them, and there's no way the band didn't know it. They simply didn't care.

The way girls raved about DD was so different from the way we boys talked about the bands we liked. I remember hours of debate in the high school lunchroom about the Clash: which was better, *London Calling* or *Sandinista!*? Is "Lover's Rock" really about oral sex? Which member of the band truly understood the geo-political context of Nicaraguan history? Who had a cooler name, Joe Strummer or Tory Crimes? My female rocker friends call this "boy list language," and they won't tolerate it. When I talk about Duran Duran with other guys, which admittedly doesn't happen all that often, we end up debating whether the Power Station was a better side project than Arcadia. No Duran Duran chick, not even the hard-core obsessives, would sit through a conversation like that.

I will always love the Clash, because I loved them so much when I was fourteen, and I love how you can start a conversation with almost literally any dude about the Clash. For instance, if you *are* a dude, you are still stuck halfway through the last paragraph, spluttering, "*London Calling* is *much* better than *Sandinista!*" This is just the way we dissect the things we love. But it's tougher to talk to women about the Clash. (They love "Stand by Me" but they don't care that it's really called "Train in Vain" instead of "Stand by Me.") So Duran Duran are a much bigger part of my day-to-day life.

I still feel like I have a lot to learn from Duran Duran. They're Zen masters on the path of infinite sluttiness, shower-nozzle heroes devoted to inspiring female fantasies. One of the things I admire about them is how they sincerely do not give a shit whether boys like them. They surrender gracefully to the female gaze. They still wear the makeup, they still dress like tarts, and every time they do a reunion tour, they play the hits they know will make the Durannies scream. They have never sold out their girls, and there's nothing about them that would evoke the dreaded words "guilty pleasure." As Oscar Wilde said, no civilized man ever regrets a pleasure, and no uncivilized man knows what a pleasure is.

The songs in this book are some of my favorite '80s relics, the songs that warped my brain with dubious ideas, boneheaded goals, laughable hopes and timeless mysteries. They might not necessarily be the greatest songs of the pre-Snooki era, or the most important, or the most popular. But they're all songs I love. And they add up to a playlist that gives a taste of that moment. In a way, you could think of these songs as Bobby Brown's pants. There's an episode of VH1's trashy reality show *Celebrity Fit Club* where everyone sits around the bonfire. They're supposed to bring some personal possession that represents the old life they're leaving behind, so they can toss it into the fire. Bobby Brown holds up a pair of baggy, sequined pants that could only come from the '80s and says, "You *know* I had to be high to buy these." (Sebastian Bach nods. He understands.) But I'm not tossing these songs into any kind of fire—I'm just shaking them to see what memories come tumbling out. And of course, a lot of those memories have to do with love, and learning about love through pop music.

It's complicated, the way we use pop culture artifacts in our day-to-day emotional relationships. The popular stereotype of this is the overbearing boyfriend who tries to get his girlfriend to appreciate free jazz, football or World War II documentaries—but everyone knows it goes both ways. Consider *Pretty Woman*, a movie that only exists so women can force their boyfriends to watch it. Your boyfriend has probably seen it more times than you have, once for every relationship. (Never more than once—unless something was seriously wrong.) And while you may kid yourself he thinks the women are hot, he's really just showing off that he's man enough to take the punishment. When you're a guy watching *Pretty Woman* with your girlfriend, you *are* Julia Roberts in the scene where Richard Gere takes her to the opera to see if she cries, because if she does, it means she's sensitive and deep and worthy to operate Richard's gear. Watching this scene on a date, you're the pretty woman, the ho on display in the opera box. And maybe you really do want to cry, if only because the supposed opera music is just the piano riff from Bruce Springsteen's "Racing in the Street."

But there's nothing at all wrong with an exchange like this. As a boy, experiences like this are part of learning girl languages.

What else is pop culture for? Since I grew up with rock-and-roll parents, bonding over the songs they loved, it never really occurred to me that love and music belonged in separate categories. When my mom and dad were growing up as 1950s rock and rollers, both sang "In the Still of the Nite" with their respective high school friends; my mom took the lead while my dad took the "shoo-doo shooby-doo" part, so they were a natural match. I'm sure that my mom and dad would find lots of other ways to bond if they didn't have music. But bringing people together is what music has always done best.

Learning to speak girl languages is a tricky business. Since I am married to an astrophysicist, I am constantly looking for ways to drop the Kuiper belt or Oort cloud into conversation. I try to impress Ally by making clever references to 3753 Cruithne, the earth's little-known "second moon," although it's more precisely described as a dynamic gravitational companion. I don't know if I impress her, but she appreciates the effort. She likes lots of '80s goth bands that I hated at the time—The Sisters of Mercy, Love and Rockets, Nitzer Ebb—but I love them now, because they're part of her language. She likes noisy, spazzy math-rock bands that only boys like, so she is also used to speaking boy languages. She's the only person I've ever met who can critique the accuracy of Google Mars as well as the Birthday Party discography.

But it's possible we will never agree on anything the way we agree on Duran Duran. Something in the music keeps promising that if I could finally figure out Duran Duran, I would finally understand women, and maybe even understand love.

Loving Duran Duran has been one of the constants in my life, but I have no idea what they would sound like if the women in my life stopped loving them. I guess I'll never know. I could claim that Duran Duran taught me everything I know about women, but that's not exactly accurate: I learned it from listening to girls talk about Duran Duran.

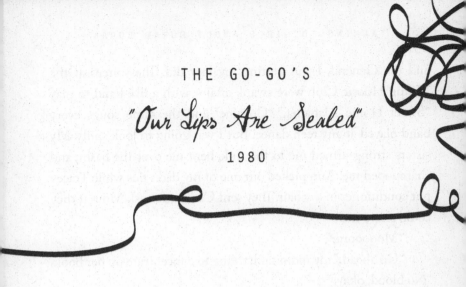

It was my first coat-and-tie dance, and I couldn't get out of it because I'd told my sisters about it. They put some serious muscle into dressing me up. All three of my sisters got in on the act—Ann was thirteen, Tracey was twelve, Caroline was only four—and even though I was the oldest at fourteen, I had no authority to say no. I was desperate to get out of the dance and do what I always did on a Friday night, which was stay home and watch *The Dukes of Hazzard*, but there was no way I was getting out of this. My sisters were intent on dolling me up. My coughing fits and "I think I've got the consumption, I mean mumps, or maybe scarlet fever" routine did nothing to fool them.

So instead of spending my quality time with Bo, Luke, Daisy

and the General, I was getting my hair did. The soirees at the Milton Hoosic Club were swank affairs, with a live band to play "Sweet Home Alabama," "Cocaine" and the same songs every band played at any teen dance. But I was going to look spiffy. My sisters strong-armed me to the sink, bent me over the basin, and shampooed me. Ann picked out one of my dad's ties while Tracey put conditioner in my hair. They sent Caroline to ask Mom if they could shave me.

"Mooooom?"

"Go ahead," my mom said, trying to concentrate on her book. "No blood, okay?"

There wasn't much legitimate stubble on my chin—I had just turned fourteen—but a few minutes later, there was foam on my face and a general consensus that debris had been cleared. Then they went for the fuzz at the back of my neck. I sat stoically while Tracey blow-dried my hair and Ann brushed it. They taught me to shine my shoes and supervised as I brushed the Cheetos dust out of my braces.

A couple hours later, I was officially dressed to kill. My sisters circled me with hand mirrors, approving their handiwork from every angle. Tracey proclaimed, "Our little baby's growing up!" Ann folded a handkerchief for the pocket square and pinned my corsage.

If I'd had a date for the dance, she might have been impressed by my slick surface. But I didn't. In fact, all I remembered about the dance was watching the band—the guitarist had a six-foot plastic tube attached to his microphone stand and a jug of Jim

Beam at his feet, so he could liquor up during the band's heartfelt rendition of Foghat's "Stone Blue." I was stone blue about missing my date with Daisy Duke.

But I knew better than to give my sisters any back talk. These were ferocious Irish girls and they drilled me well. In fact, when I saw the movie *Mean Girls*, I kept wondering when the mean girls were supposed to show up—I mean, all due respect to Lindsay Lohan and crew, but my sisters would have eaten these chicks for breakfast.

My sisters were the coolest people I knew, and still are. I have always aspired to be like them and know what they know. My sisters were the color and noise in my black-and-white boy world— how I pitied my friends who had brothers. Boys seemed incredibly tedious and dim compared to my sisters, who were always a rush of energy and excitement, buzzing over all the books, records, jokes, rumors and ideas we were discovering together. I grew up thriving on the commotion of their girl noise, whether they were laughing or singing or staging an intervention because somebody was wearing stirrup pants. I always loved being lost in that girl noise.

Yet there are so many things my sisters know about each other that I never will. They constantly laugh about private jokes I don't get, quote movies I haven't seen, nurse each other through crises they wouldn't even tell me about. They know all the symptoms when one of their kids is sick. They fight, they make up. They explode and then go right back to loving one another as fiercely as ever. It's one of the millions of secrets they share that their brother will never understand.

It's still dramatic when my sisters get together, and it always will be. In any family function, my role is to race from sister to sister saying, "She didn't mean it." It's like an opera with too many duchesses in one castle. Just a few years ago, when we were all supposed to be adults and beyond such things, my sisters kicked my mom and dad out of the house so we could have an evening at home, just us—my three sisters, their three boyfriends, and me. (One of these boyfriends was a husband.) We played board games by the fire, and perhaps a beverage or two was consumed. Then Ann mentioned the word "dollop."

This is an extremely loaded word in our family, because of an incident a few years ago when Tracey wanted to use some of Caroline's fancy shampoo, you know, *expensive* shampoo. Caroline wouldn't let Tracey use it. Not even a dollop.

"I swear, I'll only take a dollop."

"No."

"I can't have a dollop of your shampoo?"

"No."

"You can't spare a dollop? One dollop?"

"No dollops."

"Your own sister?"

Ever since the dollop incident, the word is dynamite, and nobody uses it. But on this occasion, Ann asked Caroline to pour her a dollop of Baileys. Eye contact was made, angry words were spoken, and my sisters raced upstairs to settle this matter in private. It took them about twenty minutes. They came downstairs all lovey-dovey, and we went right back to the game.

But in those twenty minutes, I sat there on the floor with all three boyfriends. I kept the conversation going—if I remember correctly, we were arguing about the U2 discography, and whether *Zooropa* was not in many ways superior to *The Joshua Tree*. The boys kept making nervous glances upstairs. I was like, "Don't look at me, dude."

In the immortal words of Keith Richards, "It's weird to be living with a bunch of chicks." But that's how I lived. To me, it seemed like a dreary waste of time not to be surrounded by bossy, zesty, loudmouthed girls. We've always been a loud family—it's fair to say that we're always the "problem table" at any wedding—and it's my sisters who pump up the volume. We like to sit at the kitchen table and talk, then drink in the living room and sing Irish songs. Mom calls out the requests for each one of us to sing, and although our voices might not get any sweeter as the night goes on, we do get louder, making up in enthusiasm what we lack in accuracy. Then we go back to the kitchen table for more talk. Since Ann and Tracey have always been tall like me, each one could talk into a different ear. I learned to take two sets of orders at the same time.

My grandmother tried explaining all this to me when I was a little boy. Nana was from County Kerry, in the old country, and she explained it was the way of our people—my sisters were always going to order me around. The Irish marry late, because they tend to starve to death if they give themselves too many mouths to feed, so the mother on an Irish farm tends to be old by the time she starts having children. That's why the eldest girl is the one who runs the farm. My grandmother was an oldest daughter, so was my mom, and so was my sister Ann. I come from a long line of Irish men who live with oldest daughters, and they basically learn to survive by washing a lot of dishes and keeping their mouths shut. My grandmother warned me that it would always be this way, but I was too young to understand. Yet meanwhile, Nana would call my sisters after school to tell them to go into the kitchen and fix me a bowl of ice cream, and maybe a milk shake with a raw egg in it for protein. And they *would*. Why?

Like any kid, I longed to be someone else, so I was fascinated by pop stars who were garish and saucy, awakening the slatternly Valley girl in my soul. I wore Psychedelic Furs and Pretenders pins on my Barracuda jacket in hopes of impressing the new-wave girl I was sure to meet any day now. Then I came home from school to watch *General Hospital* with my sisters. Dr. Noah Drake was the man—how I yearned to rock that mullet-and–lab coat look. I would have totally copped Scorpio's accent if I thought my sisters would let me get away with it. Eventually they switched to *Guiding Light*, the more mature woman's choice, but I still think of Laura, which is one of the many things I have in common with Christopher Cross.

Every day during those years, I walked to school over a tiny iron bridge blasted with graffiti dedicated to Ozzy. "Welcome to Ozzy's Coven!" it said, alongside graphic depictions of Iron Man, or maybe that was just the devil wearing a hockey helmet. Either way, it was imperative to get over the bridge before the high school kids got out of school, because then it became a place for them to blast their boom boxes, smoke, drink, get high and look for something to punch out, which was obviously where I came in. If the high school kids got to the bridge first, you had two choices: either walk a couple miles out of your way or run the gauntlet.

Across the bridge was the grassy hill that the cops set fire to every summer, because the kids had planted weed there, always a seasonal highlight for the budding pyros of my neighborhood. There was a streetlight next to the bridge that the town installed just to discourage kids from hanging out after dark, but they seemed to revel in the spotlight, blasting "More Than a Feeling" and "Cat Scratch Fever" and "Iron Man" on their radios until the cops would come chase them away. Some nights we went down by the bridge to watch the high school kids who were actually *on* the bridge, hanging out and looking cool in their own desolate honeycomb hideout, even if they were inhaling Pam out of paper bags. Ozzy and Zeppelin were singing to them, not really to me—they came to proclaim the hippie dream over and celebrate the burnout losers of the new world.

The bridge is still there, but it now looks tiny and dumpy, just a twenty-foot slab of rusted iron painted green, hardly the sort of real estate you imagine Satan and his minions would bother fighting over. But at the time, it was an epic battleground, a catwalk fraught with fright and dread and blood. I guess every American town had one of those—it was the battle of evermore.

I was the oldest kid in our house, so I was fascinated by other people's older brothers and sisters. I was thirteen when the '70s crashed into the '80s, and the prospect of all that adolescent angst stood before me like that bridge. I worshipped our babysitter, Patty, an Irish girl with red hair who took no shit from us at all. One night, my sisters and I badgered her into telling us *The Omen* as a bedtime story. She went through the whole movie scene by scene, stab wound by stab wound. I don't know how long she spent narrating the fable of Damien and his demonic conquest of the planet—maybe it took as long as it takes to watch the actual movie—but my sisters and I just screamed along, perched on the edge of the '80s.

My sisters actually got to hang out with the older girls because they were on the basketball and field hockey teams. They would shoot hoops with the basketball chicks listening to F-105, and when anyone sank a basket, they would yell "Jojo COOKIN'!" which was the inexplicably thrilling catchphrase of the ranking disco DJ in town, Jojo Kinkaid. The debate over whether Jojo was cool or not still rages on in some extremely specialized circles, but one thing is for sure: he was cookin'.

When Ann and Tracey were on the basketball team, they used to ride the bus with the older girls who blasted the radio and taught them hand dances to go with the songs. There was a hand dance for Laura Branigan's "Gloria," another for "You Should Hear How She Talks About You." I never felt more like a boy than when I was trying to learn the hand dances. Ann and Tracey tried to teach me those, but I never could crack the girlie handclap language. They would do their handclap routines, "Miss Lucy Had a Steamboat," or "Bubblegum, Bubblegum," or "The Spades Go

Two Lips Together." Every time they tried teaching me to clap along, my hands would trip over each other. I watched the girls at recess clap their hands and wondered when I would crack the code, maybe with some help from the mythical Lady with the Alligator Purse.

Rhythm was girl code, which is why I was obsessed with the claps, but I never got it right. Handclaps were the difference between boy music and girl music. Boys noticed the vocals, the guitars, while the real action was going on down below, where only girls could hear it. All my sisters' favorite songs had great handclaps, and I could never learn them. It was all I could do to learn the claps in the Cars' "My Best Friend's Girl" (CLAP clap, CLAP clap) or "Let's Go" (CLAP clap, CLAP clap clap, CLAP clap clap clap, let's go), or "Bette Davis Eyes" (clap CLAP, clap CLAP).

One time, Tracey came back from a school dance, laughing about how terribly this one guy danced. "They played 'Private Eyes,' and he was trying to clap along. He went 'Private eyes, CLAP CLAP, they're watching you, CLAP CLAP, they see your every move.'"

"Right. How is it supposed to go?"

"You know. 'Private eyes, clap CLAP, they're watching you, clap CLAP.'"

"So just the one clap then, the second time around."

"Watch. 'Private eyes. CLAP.' Now you."

"CLAP. CLAP."

"OK, now again. 'Private eyes! Clap CLAP!'"

"CLAP. CLAP CLAP."

"You know," Tracey said in her soothing tone. "You might just want to avoid the clapping-when-girls-are-around thing."

I nodded like I understood. I didn't. This was a girl language and I was on the outside. Girls can clap, boys can't. It was like the Nancy Drew book *The Clue of the Tapping Heels* where Nancy figures out the tap dancers are sending secret messages to the bad guys by tapping in Morse code.

When you're a kid, every step in identity is marked by a step in music. You were totally defined by which station you listened to, graduating from the kiddie station to the teenybop station to the grown-up stations. In our house, the radio was always on, whether it was my parents' doo-wop and oldies, the weekend Irish drinking songs on WROL or me and my sisters trying to navigate our own way around the dial. WRKO was AM Top 40 for girls. F-105 was FM Top 40 for seventh and eighth grade girls or sixth grade boys. Kiss-108 was disco for girls or very secure boys. WBZ and WHDH were pop for parents. WBCN ("the Rock of Boston") was rock for arty kids. WCOZ was like WBCN, but heavier and not as arty. It ran ads proclaiming "Kick Ass Rock & Roll!" or "WCOZ . . . [painful grunt] . . . the Rock & Roll MUTHA!" I believe the Mutha set a broadcasting record by playing "Whole Lotta Love" continuously for six years straight.

There was a lot of radio out there, and I didn't want to miss any of it. In seventh grade, I switched from WRKO to F-105 to WCOZ in the space of six months. By eighth and ninth grade, it was WBCN. Tenth grade introduced WHTT, the new contemporary hits radio station, which played nothing but Toni Basil's "Mickey" and Musical Youth's "Pass the Dutchie." There was always Magic 106, with a heavy-breathing seductive DJ named David Allan Boucher who was always hosting *Bedtime Magic*, the show where he would recite the lyrics of the songs in his very sexy way, as a soundtrack to what must have been the most depressing adult sex imaginable.

Top 40 radio was a constant education in the ways of the world. I learned what sex was from Barry White appearing on *The Mike Douglas Show* to sing "It's Ecstasy When You Lay Down Next to Me." Barry himself, looking fine in a green velour leisure suit, wandered out into the crowd to preach a little sermon as the band vamped on the bassline. "Is this song about one person? Is this song about three people? No! It's about two people. Yeah. Two people." I was grateful to the Round Mound of Sound for every scrap of wisdom he could throw me.

One of our favorite songs was Sister Sledge's disco classic "We Are Family," still all over the radio in 1980, getting played like it was a brand-new hit even though it dated back to the summer of 1979. Our baby sister, Caroline, a decade younger than me but picking up all of our cool music in the timeless tradition of sassy little sisters throughout human history, loved to sing along with this one, making up her own words: "We are family! We got all the sisters we need!" Those are still my favorite words to that song, because (in our case) they were true. But it's funny how this song never goes away, and every generation of baby sisters puts their own spin on it. Just the other day, in a movie theater lobby outside the Harry Potter movie, I heard a little Puerto Rican girl singing it as "We are family! Yeah, Mama, sing it to me!" And she was singing it to a life-size cardboard cutout of Megan Fox, which only proves there is no limit to the Sledge sisterhood.

Rick Springfield from *General Hospital* had started making hard rock records, and although they were theoretically guitar rock records for boys, they were the girliest thing ever, and I was vaguely threatened by how much I loved them. I felt so dirty when Rick Springfield sang cute, but as Rick would say, the point is probably moot. "Jessie's Girl" turned out to be one of the '80's most enduring hits. Hell, in the Rite Aid in my neighborhood, teen girls can still buy Jesse's Girl Baked Powder Eye Shadow, which is stocked on the shelf right next to the Love's Baby Soft and Hannah Montana Glamour Guitar Lollipops.

I thrilled to the glories of rock-and-roll radio, especially the Doors. Was any band ever so perfectly designed for teenage boys? My friends and I were typical eighth grade dorks at the time, in that our sex education mostly took the form of Jim Morrison. We studied *No One Here Gets Out Alive* as if it were holy writ, and memorized the entire soliloquy in "The End," right down to the chilling "he walked on down the hall" conclusion. They seemed more like an '80s new-wave combo than a classic rock legend, in part because they clearly had no idea what they were doing and didn't even bother faking it. They prepared me for all the nightmarishly pretentious and incompetent new wave that would become my adolescent raison d'etre. The Doors revival was in full swing, with the immortal *Rolling Stone* cover that showed Jim Morrison with the words "He's hot, he's sexy and he's dead." (I was 0 for 3 in that department.)

Can you blame us? When you're an eighth grade boy, everything sucks in your life *except* Jim Morrison. We felt Jim was a god—or at least a lord—who had faked his death and escaped to Africa. When he returned, he would reward our faith, telling us, "Well done, thou good and faithful servants." Eventually, we started to get the sinking feeling that even if Morrison did fake his death, he probably died later anyway, and we never heard about it. But that's too depressing to think about. Morrison lives! What was it Jim Morrison said? "People are strange, when you're a stranger"? More like "People impose, when you're a poseur."

I assumed my sisters would scoff at the Doors, but Tracey ended up doing a book report on *No One Here Gets Out Alive*. We were always checking out each other's music, books, magazines, everything, looking to surprise each other with new kinds of fun. One day I put on the cassette of *Jesus Christ Superstar* only to find that Tracey had taped something new over it: the Go-Go's album *Beauty and the Beat*. I grieved for a few minutes before I realized I was now off the hook and never had to listen to that annoying, bogus show-tune church shit *ever again*. Praise Jesus!

And praise the Go-Go's. Man, we listened to that tape over and over again. Every song sounded like it was the chronicle of a world that was much cooler than the '70s burnout rock we heard all around us. It was a report from California, where sassy girls got dressed up and messed up and went out to cool places to do evil. "This town is our town," they sang. "It is so glamorous! Bet you'd live here if you could and be one of us!"

I used to dream about being the only boy in the Go-Go's. I

had to feel like that was the ultimate rock-star gig. I had the scenario all planned out, that I would learn to play bass and replace Kathy Valentine. (Sorry, Kathy!) I would be Jane Wiedlin's true love, and she would take me to wherever she got her hair did and fix me up a little, because I wasn't really presentable enough to hit cool places with her. Our lips would be sealed. I would get to borrow her stripey pants and sing backup on my favorite Go-Go's song, "How Much More," which was basically just the two words "girl" and "tonight" repeated over and over. Since those are the two new-waviest words in the English language, it was brilliant to give them their own song. I would rewind this song over and over, close my eyes and dream of being one of the girls. I want to be that girl tonight. Girl tonight!

I'm still in awe of my sisters. The only thing I would even consider changing about them is that their husbands are taller than I am. (We've had words about that.) But I would love to know anything as deeply as they know one another. I'll never get their ability to laugh for hours over nothing, but I crave being part of their girl noise even when I don't understand it.

What I don't get, they are more than willing to teach. I am always learning new rules from them. Giving compliments, for example—always a good idea, yet there are rules for doing it right. My sisters taught me to start with the shoes, and then keep the compliments coming. Never compliment her eyes, because that means she thinks you think she's plain. Always compliment something else before you compliment the hair, but always compliment the hair. If you're giving a compliment you don't mean, which is often advisable, sandwich it between a couple that you *do* mean. My sisters had a *lot* of rules.

Everything was changing so fast and moving in stereo. My voice was breaking, so I creaked from Andy Gibb highs to Isaac Hayes lows in the space of a single syllable, even when the syllable was "uuuuh." I was saying it *and* spraying it, thanks to my brand-new braces. I was growing so rapidly that I had to relearn how to walk every few months, bumping into trees and tripping over my feet on such a regular basis, inspiring the classic greeting, "Smooth move, Ex-Lax." Nothing could really help me make sense out of my spindly, gangly body and all the hormones exchanging gunfire in it. Nothing, that is, except my radio.

My sisters did their best with me. Music helped.

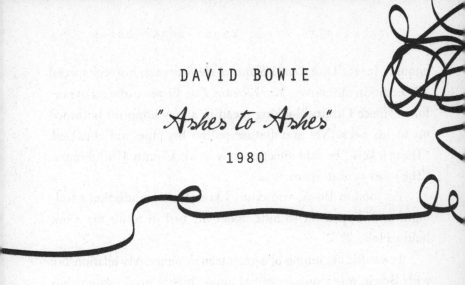

DAVID BOWIE

"Ashes to Ashes"

1980

David Bowie ended life as I knew it one Sunday morning, entering my life the way a true prophet should—over a bowl of Fruity Pebbles. After church, I was waiting for my sisters to get done with the funnies, perusing *Parade*. There was a question in "Walter Scott's Personality Parade." "Does David Bowie dye his hair, and is he gay?" Mr. Scott responded, "David Bowie, who dyes his hair orange and claims to come from Mars, is reportedly bisexual."

I never made it to the funnies. I had no idea what either "reportedly" or "bisexual" meant, but I knew now that rock and roll was as sinister and excellent as I always feared it was.

I first got a look at the man in rock-star mode at my grandparents' house on the last night of the 1970s, appropriately enough. It was *Dick Clark's Salute to the Seventies*, his very special 1979 edition of the *New Year's Rockin' Eve*. Bowie came on to perform "Space Oddity," looking mean in a gray jumpsuit buttoned up to his neck. My grandfather puffed his pipe and chuckled. "These jokers," he said affectionately in his County Cork brogue. "The joker is from space, is he?"

As soon as Bowie was done, I kissed my grandfather goodnight and slipped off to hide under my bed in terror for a few hours. Hello, '80s!

It was the beginning of a great teen romance. My relationship with Bowie was a quintessential junior high school relationship, with the caveat that he knew nothing about it. I kept breaking up with him, staging tearful reunions, having worrisome fits over "Where is this headed?" and "Do we have anything in common?" often renouncing him entirely and vowing to listen to nothing except hard-core punk or folk music or whatever was turning my head that week, only to realize there was no getting away from Bowie. It was like trying to break up with the color orange, or Wednesday, or silent *e*. It was the most passionate and tumultuous relationship I'd ever known.

I was full of complicated romantic feelings at this time. I was pretty sure I was madly in love, but had no idea with whom or what—I had it narrowed down to the girls' JV squash team, but that's not too helpful, and between *Dynasty* and *T.J. Hooker*, Heather Locklear was only on TV two nights a week, so what was a boy to do? Since I was ferociously pursuing a rigorous course in dimly understood Catholic devotion, I carried a safety pin in my pocket to jab myself in the event of carnal desires, to prevent them from happening, yet this was a defense mechanism that proved useless—it didn't even get me through algebra class, not with Holly Greene sitting in front of me. That girl knew how to pronounce the word "parabola."

I would come home from school and do my Latin homework in my room, stretched out on my Boston Bruins sleeping bag, with Wacky Packages stuck to every flat surface and pictures of rock stars taped up all over the wall. My *Star Wars* posters faced off as Bowie's voice whispered over the tape deck to fill up the room. He made the space seem impossibly glamorous. I got to know his voice well, as he translated sexual confusions and cravings into the absurd romantic pageant I knew they were supposed to be, and he made it a lot less lonely.

I yearned to become the Thin White Duke, yet I was stuck being a Thin White Douche. I studiously imitated his every move. There were so many Bowies I could barely keep track of them, but somehow the Bowie I liked best was the one from right now. The way he looked, sounded and moved reminded me of C-3PO. Except not as cheerful. Sometimes he was a heavy-breathing rock stud, like in "Rebel Rebel." Sometimes he was a disco queen, like in "Fame." Sometimes he was a crooner straight from *The Lawrence Welk Show*, sometimes he was Dracula with a head cold, sometimes he was a clown with an eye patch. Sometimes he was a lonely space traveler stuck on earth, doomed to wander around in disguise without ever finding a home, kind of like the Incredible Hulk. ("Don't make me sexy! You wouldn't like me when I'm sexy!")

Whoever he was, he made everything different. When his song is playing, that's not just a radio—it's Ground Control, picking up signals and random messages floating in from outer space. And you're not a loser spending Friday night at home with the radio—you're experiencing a night full of star-crossed romance and serious moonlight. He sang about girls in space—why not? That's where all the cool girls were. (They weren't where I could find them, that was for sure.)

He created a night world of new romantics and modern lovers, populated by all the bizarre creatures he sang about. He was a kindly presence, a cracked pastor for all of us moonage daydream believers, pretty things and hot tramps, queen bitches and slinky vagabonds, people from bad homes, night crawlers and pinups and young dudes and scary monsters. They moved in numbers and they plotted in corners. And you could join them just by listening. The *B* section of the local record store is where you'd find them. I started to spend many afternoons loitering around the *B*s.

True, it was somewhat unlikely the astral-traveling rebel chick of my dreams would show up at the Popcorn Records at the South Shore Plaza in Braintree, Massachusetts, sprinkle some stardust on me, and invite me to go on a "Young Americans" bus ride through the existential highways of our youth. But you never knew, right? It's not like I had other plans. And waiting for her to stumble out of a Bowie song was a lot easier than attempting to go out and search for her, which was frankly out of the question for a tongue-tied trollop-in-training like me.

This was the era when Pat Benatar had just become a huge star, and in response, the Massachusetts State Legislature had issued a decree that no female between the ages of twelve and forty could leave the house without a killer headband-and-leotard combo. (It was still a couple years before the landmark Leg Warmer Bylaws of spring '83.) But the new-wave girl was out there. I was sure of that. I would recognize her because she would have torn her dress and her face would be a mess. She'd take pity on my shaggy hair and Barracuda jacket and Toughskin pants, and she'd recognize me as a kindred spirit. She might teach me something about fashion, or at least dress me up a little, shine a little of her glimmer on me. Bowie was going to guide me to her world.

Bowie became my obsession. Bowieism and futurism and the whole new-wave mythology he invented were a way of life that seemed hunky-dory to me. I couldn't get tickets when he played at Boston's Sullivan Stadium, but I listened faithfully on WBCN as the DJ consoled those of us who were shut out from the concert with an all-night Bowie marathon. Sometime after midnight, a couple of other DJs came to the studio, straight from Sullivan Stadium, gibbering like kids about how excellent he was and how they got backstage and looked into his eyes and they really were *two different colors.* Then they announced they had a cigarette butt that they'd stolen out of Bowie's ashtray, and they were going to ceremoniously *light it up* and *smoke it* on the air. Did I keep listening? Yes, I did. I probably had a better time than my friend Josh, who went to the show with his big sisters and tried to rise to the occasion by dyeing his hair orange. Some older rock dude saw him in the hot dog line and snickered, "Hey clown, what's up?" I still think about that. I like to think a real citizen of Bowie World would never be that mean.

Bowie's big radio hit that eighth grade year was "Ashes to Ashes," which was his sequel to "Space Oddity," revisiting the story of Major Tom. (Rock stars are allowed to do that? Isn't that cheating?) Bowie sounded like his voice was changing, like mine. He mumbled and wailed, as if he were stuck somewhere very frightening indeed, but had no idea how to get back home, like he'd missed the 7:20 bus from the Plaza. By the end, he was screaming, "I want to come down right now!" But Major Tom doesn't get to come down, he's still up there floating, and this time nobody's listening and nobody mourns him.

"Ashes to Ashes" is Bowie's most famous video—it's an acclaimed work of art, one I've seen exhibited at the Museum of Modern Art. But there was no MTV back then, so "Ashes to Ashes" was only a radio hit. The one time I saw the video at the time was on *Entertainment Tonight*, and it scared the bejeezus out of me. Bowie is a sad clown on the beach, apparently agitated by a little sand in his tights, walking under a bloodred sky with a bunch of goth priests and priestesses. He strolls the beach with an old lady who looked remarkably like my grandmother. He also walks in front of a bulldozer, which I guessed must symbolize harvesting the crops of awesome.

I decided I knew exactly what this song was about. Bowie was clearly suffering "cold turkey" withdrawal from drug addiction, a topic I knew well from watching TV. Starsky and Hutch had to deal with this shit all the time. You know the *Baretta* episode where

Lawrence Hilton-Jacobs is a junkie? And his dad Whitman Mayo gets accused of killing the drug dealer? Well, I knew the word "junkie" from this episode, so Bowie couldn't slip a thing past me. Bowie was going through cold turkey, like Gene Hackman in *The French Connection II*. Gene Hackman demands they lock him in a room so he can suffer and sweat and scream, and that they bring him nothing except cheeseburgers with extra onions. So heroin always reminds me of onions. (I don't like onions at all, which may be why I've steered clear of hard drugs.)

For those of us who were too young to be doing drugs and dyeing our hair orange at the time, this was a prophecy of the future. Not in terms of fashion—the pyramid-on-head look? Impractical. Ziggy Stardust's loincloth? Too Pampers. The Pierrot constume as beachwear? As Tim Gunn might say, that's a lot of look, David. We need you to go upstairs and clean out your space, okaaay?

Even a rabid Bowie freak has to be a little weirded out that the whole "Bowie's in space" thing is still such a huge hit, such an inescapable cultural presence, after all this time. Major Tom is still totally famous, despite the fact that nobody gives a crap about real-life astronauts anymore. By now, he's the *only* famous astronaut there is, unless you count Buzz Aldrin, who was famous enough to (1) go on *Punky Brewster* after the *Challenger* explosion and tell Punky it was still okay to want to be an astronaut when she grew up, and (2) go on *The Rosie O'Donnell Show* to recite the lyrics of "Rocket Man."

The story of Major Tom keeps getting rewritten—for the story so far, see Elton John's "Rocket Man," Peter Schilling's "Major

Tom (Coming Home)," Joy Division's "Disorder," U2's "Bad," Neil Young's "After the Gold Rush," Black Sabbath's "Supernaut," and so many more. Lou Reed turned it into "Satellite of Love," while Depeche Mode turned it into "satellite of hate." The best scene in any Adam Sandler movie is when he takes his first helicopter ride in *Mr. Deeds* and leads the cast in a sing-along of "Space Oddity." Cat Power can do her acoustic version of it in a car commercial, and nobody even thinks that's strange. Like you'd ever want to be in a car driven by Major Tom! They'd never find your car again! Your GPS would simply read, "I think my spaceship knows which way to go" and then poof, you're gone!

Practically every Major Tom song is great—who doesn't love "Rocket Man"? (Besides Bowie, that is?) I think it's just because everybody knows what it's like to be crushed out on satellites. And when Peter Schilling sang "Major Tom (Coming Home)," about feeling so lost and confused on earth that you just want to blast off to your own private planet and be a pop star on your own private screen, leaving all the earth girls behind, I knew exactly what he was singing about too. Like Patti Smith says, "Okay, earth boys— you had your chance."

The man has often stated he was out of his mind on drugs for much of this period; he claims he can't even remember making his best album, *Station to Station*, and he's cheerfully admitted, "I honestly have no idea what I thought between 1975 and 1977." What we do know is that at some point, the universe said, "Mr. Bowie, meet cocaine. Cocaine, Bowie. Get acquainted, you two!" And so it came to pass that Bowie spent a ridiculous amount of his golden years gadding about L.A. like a blond coat hanger with a dead rock star hanging on it.

The blow-and-shoulder-pads days were strange even for Bowie: going on *The Dinah Shore Show* with Henry Winkler ("I'm a great fan of Fonzie"), singing "Song Sung Blue" on TV with Cher, even appearing on the Grammy Awards to present an award to Aretha Franklin, who proclaimed, "I'm so happy, I could kiss David Bowie!"

There's no doubt Bowie was one fucked-up rock star then. He went through a powder-brained period of talking up fascism, as if any self-respecting fascist would be caught dead marching beside David Bowie. Like all English people his age, he was besotted by hilarious superstitions, embodied in the quintessentially English figure of Aleister Crowley, who wouldn't be one of the ten weirdest people in my apartment building but somehow symbolized evil and decadence for all the English rock stars of the '70s. It's odd because Crowley just looks like Willard Scott, except nowhere near as scary. Come on, what's more demonic—living in a castle and wearing a Sphinx costume or going on nationwide TV to predict the weather and talk dirty to hundred-year-old ladies?

But even if Bowie was crazy, dangerous and utterly baleful in every aspect of his influence on my impressionable little brain, I learned a lot from him. Even at his most out-there space-trippy, he's making the case for earth. Even Ziggy, his most glitzily self-destructive concept project, ends with a big ballad that's explicitly antisuicidal, insisting that you shouldn't destroy yourself or cower from life, you should just find somebody as fucked-up as you to love (or at least be nice to), so you can treat each other like you're rock-and-roll stars. He seemed to say, *you're not alone*, since there are millions of other pathetic freakazoids out there, and the *B* section of the record store is where you will find them hanging out, so get cracking. Give one another compliments like "You're wonderful" or "You're a total blam blam" or whatever it is slutty Martians say to one another.

When I hear him sing "Ashes to Ashes," he sounds scared, but he also sounds like the golden years are just beginning, because he knows the sky is full of lovesick space cadets like him or you or me, if you just care enough to notice them. And the stars look very dif-fer-ent today.

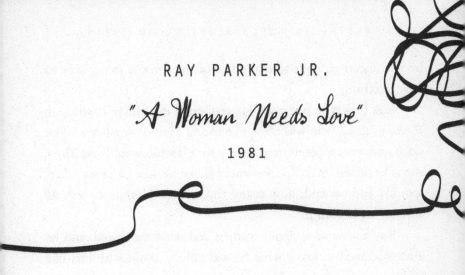

"A Woman Needs Love"

1981

Why do we look to pop singers to tell us how to be boyfriends? I wish I knew, but we do. I still do—even though pop singers are probably the least qualified people on earth when it comes to such matters. Monogamous musicians are like vegan hockey players. But Ray Parker Jr., he was serving up boyfriend lessons on a monthly basis.

"A Woman Needs Love" kept humming out of the speakers at Houghton's Pond, where my sisters and I went to swim. Since my voice was changing, singing along was a challenge—I would pick either my tenor or baritone and try to push it all the way through. My sisters thought it was hilarious, but one of the things I liked about Ray Parker Jr. is he didn't sound like he was mean enough to make fun of me for not being able to sing like him.

Ray Parker Jr. was cool. He reminded me of Mr. Rourke on *Fantasy Island*, who was always lecturing Tattoo on what women want and what women need. Every time Tattoo would say, "Boss, she is beautiful," Mr. Rourke would shake his head and say, "Tattoo, my little friend, how many times must I remind you? *All* women are beautiful!"

Ray always sang about women and what they need, and he always seemed to know what he was talking about with hits like "A Woman Needs Love." He schooled me in my duty to the ladies of the world, because women need love and ask for lots and lots of it and it is in your selfish interest to satisfy their stupid whims and careless demands. If you cannot supply their needs, they will find various other men to supply the various needs you are not meeting. I was shocked at Ray's scenario: "One day you might come home early from work, open up the door and get your feelings hurt." I had a vague idea of what that might look like, and it wasn't good.

Ray never stressed, though. He did not sweat the technique. He wasn't exactly a high-strung diva or even a megafamous pop star—he was what serious *Match Game* fans call a "fourth seater," the guy taking up the pivotal chair between Charles Nelson Reilly and Richard Dawson. You don't want a chatty comedian in that spot (that's the first seat) or a glamorous sitcom starlet (the sixth seat), just someone exuding a quiet charm and warmth to keep the game moving.

That was RPJ. He ministered to his flock of suburban

swimming-pool acolytes who hung on his every word and shuddered at his parables of the Eternal Feminine. He stayed relaxed through it all. He reminded me of my grandfather, who'd sit there puffing his pipe while my grandmother ranted and raved. Then she'd ask him, "Are you over it?" and he'd nod. Then they'd go back to normal and he'd do some dishes.

In the news, Jimmy Carter had just gone to Poland and inadvertently caused a crisis because his interpreter bungled his Polish speeches—Jimmy told the bewildered crowds that he "lusted" for their country, and that he had left America "never to return." It was not a successful diplomatic mission. The Polish premier Edward Gierek later reportedly said, "I had to grit my teeth from time to time. But one must not be rude to ladies or interpreters." That seemed like something Ray or Mr. Rourke would say.

We go to pop singers to hear such extravagant bended-knee submisson to the female will—we learn from our advice-mongering studs on the microphone. And we will ourselves into believing they have any idea what they're talking about. I have read Smokey Robinson's autobiography, which is admirably frank on his swinging sex life, and I cannot help but think of how much I depended on Smokey Robinson to teach me how to be a boyfriend, a suitor, a husband. Just in the way he sings "ooo" in the chorus of "Ooo Baby Baby," he taught me tons about how to be erotically bereaved, how to suffer for romantic choices poorly made, mistakes regretted, opportunities unwisely seized, reconnections that aren't possible. The lyric is just a rough sketch telling you why the "ooo" is in the song, but nobody really needs it—it's all there in the "ooo." He taught me to be miserable suffering for a woman, and how to love every minute of it. But even after reading Smokey Robinson's autobiography, and learning that he spent the "Tracks of My Tears" years getting more ass than a tour-bus driver's seat, I still take a seminar from him on bending to the will of women every time I hear him whimper "You Really Got a Hold on Me" or moan through "Baby, Baby Don't Cry."

In his own way, Ray Parker Jr. is one of these musical sages of love. "A Woman Needs Love" was a hit that made me ponder my duties to women. Although I was only a boy, I was getting a sense of the ever-increasing list of services I would be called upon to provide, outside of those contained in various soul songs.

Reaching things in high places

I was about eight when old ladies began coming up to me in the supermarket and telling me to reach things for them. How did they know I would? They just knew.

Consuming food

This has always been a tough one. The desire of women to see men enjoy their food is one I have always found a challenge. My grandmother's desire to fatten me up makes sense, given that she came from a rural Irish area plagued by famine and influenza, but it went deeper than that. My sisters always found it amusing when she would call and order them to feed me—yet now they have the same obsession with feeding their own sons. We're not really sure how this happened.

Knowing what slingbacks are
A type of shoe. If you ask if she's wearing slingbacks, the answer is usually no, but the effort is seldom wasted.

Walking to cars
I was twenty-one the first time. I was walking home from the Grotto in New Haven, where I had just been moshed into a bloody pulp. The girls behind me were yelling, "Hey, green shirt! Walk us to our car!" So I did. They were parked in a bad neighborhood, as were all the neighborhoods in that town. When we got to the car, I wondered for a crazy second whether they were going to offer me a ride, but they weren't dumb. This same scene played out at about two-thirds of the rock shows I attended in that city.

Saving a seat
I thought this was just my first girlfriend, but it turned out to be every girlfriend. I do not have what you would call a "seat-saving personality," i.e., I am nowhere near chatty enough to keep having the same two-line conversation with fifty people ("Yes, someone's sitting here. She'll be right back.") in the three or four minutes before the band goes on or the movie starts. This is one of my designated areas for improvement.

Opening things with lids
And then saying, "You loosened it up for me."

Checking the expiration dates
Salad dressing? Expires after about a week. Never gets
thrown away. Every time I'm in my mom's kitchen, I end up
raiding the cabinets, searching for canned or bottled goods
that have piled up years after they presumably went bad.

Singing Irish songs
Every year on my mom's birthday, I call her and sing "Bold
Thady Quill," an Irish song we love to share because it's one
that nobody else seems to like. When we sit around the fire
singing Irish songs for my mom, my brother-in-law John
takes the long sad songs with plots, because he actually has
a voice. I just sing the ones about drunken hurlers and wild
rovers. Either way, singing for the women in our family is a
sacred duty.

Asking if she got a haircut
If someone I knew asked me this question every other week,
I would think there was something wrong with their cogni-
tive process. But for some reason, asking this question never
seems to come as an annoyance or a surprise. From across
the room, you can just mime a pair of scissors and give a
thumbs-up.

Beating up mean people
An offer always appreciated, though seldom taken up on, and
blatantly insincere coming from me. The only times I have

been called upon to actually do this were at a pro-choice rally in 1989 where we got attacked by right-to-lifers, and a Sleater-Kinney show in 1996 where I successfully threw out two tough guys and then wouldn't shut up about it for weeks.

Counting the ply

On a roll of toilet paper, there is fine print at the very bottom of the package, with the suffix "ply." The prefix is either the numeral 1 or the numeral 2. If you pick 1, you have made a decision you will regret a little or a lot, depending on whoever is back at home waiting for the toilet paper.

Not asking how they met their boyfriends

Most women *love* to tell this story, and indeed can't keep still about it. But if you've known a couple for forty-five minutes, and the woman still hasn't brought it up, it means they met at a party when she got drunk and blew him in the bathroom to make her ex-boyfriend mad. She does *not* want to talk about it. (He does, but not around her.) (And her ex is probably talking about it right now, but that's someone else's problem.)

Making conversation with their boyfriends

Female friends' boyfriends are either in bands or they're not. If her boyfriend is not in a band, it's easy to talk to him. Just mention two geographical areas, and you will discuss the various ways to get from one to the other. You're from New

Hampshire? Okay, Guadalajara. How do you get there? Do you take the Tappan Zee Bridge? Stay off I-95? I don't know why, but for males, this seems to top politics or sports or music or any other topic. As long as you stick to "ways to get somewhere from somewhere else," talking to boyfriends is a snap.

If he's in a band, it's a lot harder to be polite. It requires turning up at one of his shows now and then. It requires nodding and saying, "You don't sound *that* much like Joy Division. More like early Can." It requires paying for his drinks and not rolling your eyes when he claims he left his wallet in the guitar case. But it's important to keep exposure time brief, because after ten minutes it becomes impossible not to laugh out loud when he claims he sounded this way long before anyone had heard of Animal Collective. At that point, you've done your duty for your friend; she will be grateful you tried.

You can now be as mean to him as you like. He has no idea you're being mean, because (1) he's not listening to a word you say, and (2) he has no idea he's her boyfriend.

The list goes on, gets longer every year. It never ends. It never gets any shorter. There is always more required of you. That's another thing Ray Parker Jr. was trying to tell me.

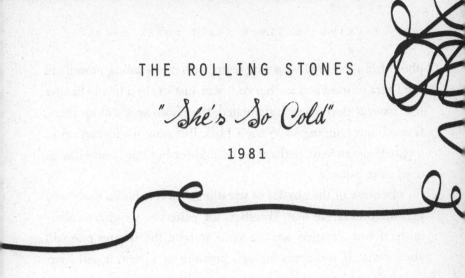

My wrestling career record was 0–14, yet I racked up a few moral victories. For instance, there were matches where none of my vertebrae snapped, and a few times there were no loud crunching noises. My mom came to see me wrestle once, and apologized for never being able to go back. I don't blame her. No Irish mother should ever have to witness her firstborn getting bodyslammed while wearing a plastic mouthguard.

I was a resounding success at wrestling, compared to my utter failure to explain to anyone I've met since high school why I was allowed on the wrestling team. When I took my wife, Ally, back to visit my old school, there were all sorts of places I wanted to show her. But the main thing I wanted to show her was the team photo from the 1981 wrestling team, with me beaming proudly in my Lycra unitard and leather codpiece, just so she'd finally believe me. I swear that when I graduated, the photo was still up there, framed and hanging in Warren Hall. But now it's locked up in a closet somewhere, perhaps to be sold for big bucks on eBay or used as an ashtray.

Because of the physics of wrestling, I never should have been permitted near the mat. Wrestlers are paired by weight, so obviously, if two wrestlers are the same weight, the shorter one will always win. If you apply enough pressure to a joint, it will snap, so it helps to have a thick, square, blocklike build, preferably with no joints at all. I was very tall, bony, stretched out like a sweatsock that had just been used as a gorilla condom, with a long neck that was easily laced into a full Windsor. Every wrestler my weight was built like a minifridge, so it was literally impossible for me to win a match unless I packed a nunchaku, or unless I pulled out the easily concealed and widely advertised Kiyoga: the Steel Cobra. I was below featherweight, bantamweight, chickenweight—somewhere near a shameweight.

Oddly, this is one of the few areas in my life where I was brimming with confidence, if only because there was no pressure to win. Indeed, if I lasted the whole match and lost on points, instead of getting pinned immediately, my teammates would slap me on the back as if I'd crushed a man with my bare hands. I had never been so extravagantly proud of having blood that clotted. Wrestling was to my teen years what karaoke became to my adulthood—a pursuit where I had no skill but total enthusiasm and full commitment, a performance ritual where I felt completely devoid of shame.

This wrestling was not like "pro wrestling," which was big on television at the time but still a few years away from exploding into the mass entertainment juggernaut it has become, to the point where my dad would take my little sister to Boston Garden to see the stars stomp each other's tracheas. Our team did not have colorful stage names or flamboyant personalities, nor were we permitted to jump from any lighting fixtures. I guess it was kind of a transitional period in terms of male-combat culture. Spiritually, we were trapped in the odd historical vacuum between *Rocky II* and *Rocky III*. Rocky was still the world heavyweight champion—he hadn't lost his crown, wept at Mickey's deathbed, been pitied by Mr. T. He had not regained the eye of the tiger. We had no way of knowing Apollo Creed was going to help him rise up to the challenge of his rival, much less that Rocky was going to eventually knock out Ivan Drago, Tommy Gunn, or Mason "The Line" Dixon. The jury was still out on this Balboa meathead. He would have been a great role model, but as it was, I had to face this battle on my own and don my tights of redemption-scented Lycra.

My coach, Steel Neil Coughlin, was a stoic about it, since he had no way to boot me from the junior varsity team—there was no level lower than JV, and I was equally unsuited for the other winter sports. Squash was fun, but in the winter the courts belonged to the varsity. Basketball was always a drag for me, as it is for most fifteen-year-olds who are six feet tall yet unable to throw things. My sisters, who were built like me, absolutely killed at volleyball, so I tried it once, and then I saw stars and that was the end of that. When I was a junior, my school introduced badminton, which was clearly a P.E. department ploy to get me away from the wrestling room, and it worked, since the first time I played badminton was like the first time I tasted sushi or heard the Beatles or read Wordsworth. *This* was a sport? This counted for gym requirements? "Pleased to meet you, badminton," I told the shuttlecock. "Hope you guessed my name." But at this point, the badminton team was just a gleam in Steel Neil's increasingly exasperated eye.

At that age, any physical activity vaguely resembling sexual contact is hilarious. But there's nothing vague about wrestling. It begins with one dude on hands and knees, as the other one wraps an arm around to nestle against his chest (the "upside-down belt hold") and another arm on his elbow. Then they roll around on the rubber mat. A wrestling match will often involve a friction boner or two. So a serious attitude is a must. Otherwise, you'll just giggle and miss the more difficult pleasures available to the true wrestler. The varsity wrestling team, who used the practice room after we did, were very serious guys, and it was inspiring to watch them stretch for hours while we rehearsed our falls and clinches. There's no denying that there was an element of showing off for these guys. The varsity team was undefeated, feared throughout the Independent School League. I hope it was inspirational to watch us warm up the mat for them, falling down in incredibly complicated ways.

At practice, I always paired up with my buddy Flynn, who had a similarly Zen approach to the sport, derived from *Kung Fu* reruns on Channel 38. We were fascinated with the strategy of combat, the chesslike logical quandaries, the questions of leverage and balance. It was yogic, in a way, even if I was the kind of yogi whose lotus position was two shoulders to the mat. We loved the uniform and the ritual of lacing up the boots. As adolescent boys who loved martial arts mythology but were too lazy to actually learn any martial arts, wrestling suited our warrior-philosopher fantasies.

Flynn and I were well matched physically and cerebrally, so the time we spent with our faces in proximity facilitated our philosophical discussions.

"You know what would suck?" he mused one day as we grappled on the leather mat, standing face to face for the clinch.

"What would suck?"

"In *1984*, if Winston Smith was afraid of squirrels instead of rats."

We were reading George Orwell in English class, and since we were the Class of '84, we identified heavily with its dystopian vision.

"Why would that suck?"

"That would render him laughable. It wouldn't be horrible when they show him rats in Room 101. It would just be funny."

"True," I conceded, scoring reversal points on the half nelson. "That would suck."

"The torture guys would probably just laugh."

"Even the squirrels would laugh. Winston's resistance to evil would have meant nothing."

"It would doubleplus suck."

We dropped to our knees to execute the Olympic lift.

"This is all true," I said. "Yet I cannot help but feel that what would really suck would be living in that futuristic totalitarian society. In fact, I think it's a little strange, and maybe disturbing, you come away from the novel thinking that's what would suck."

"Or rabbits."

"What about hamsters?"

"That would suck too."

He slipped his arms into the forbidden full nelson. I nudged him away with my jaw.

"What about cats?"

"Not as much as rabbits."

"Bats. That would be awesome."

"Awesome."

"What do you call a masturbating cow?"

"Beef stroganoff."

Splaaat! Pinned. Again.

Wrestling team was my first experience riding in vans with groups of other boys who were all dressed alike. It was extremely exciting. Not surprising, since we were guys, we argued over music in the van, with the usual battle of rock versus disco. Doug Martilla had the boom box, and everyone had a different idea of what constituted proper psych-up music for the match ahead of us. Jose from the Bronx, the first kid I ever saw breakdance in real life, brought salsa tapes to get the testosterone pumping. He was serious, and clearly bound for varsity next year. The kid who brought in Yes was clearly killing time till Frisbee season. One kid always insisted on The Who's *Quadrophenia*, which suggests a self-sabotaging sense of doom.

The tape everyone could agree on was the Stones. Jose pointed out the congas in "Sympathy for the Devil," but *Hot Rocks* had too many slow songs, so it always ended up being the Maxell C-90 tape with *Emotional Rescue* on one side and *Tattoo You* on the other. "She's So Cold," that was the jam. Mick Jagger sang like he was a hot girl, so it was odd how perfect he was at psyching us up for a wrestling match. Mick Jagger was a skinny-guy role model for me, at a time when it was not acceptable to be skinny—those were the days of Soloflex Man posters and Nautilus ads. My bone structure would have been an undeniable asset if I'd been a future Eastern European tranny underwear model, yet it was a stigma for a high school boy in that time and place. It was embarrassing to have other people see my shoulders, arms or legs. But in wrestling drag, my body was invisible, because I was in character. All anyone could see was the unitard of valor.

Or at least that's how I perceived it. Of course, at any match, the other team across the room would see me on the bench, and eagerly check the coach's clipboard to see which one of them got *that* kid. I never had to check Mr. Coughlin's clipboard, because I could always tell the guy who was paired up with me—he was the one sitting on the bench, salivating, twitching his knee because he could barely wait for his turn to get out there. He had that delirious look in his eye. You know in the cartoons when Bugs Bunny gets trapped in the desert, starved for food, so then he looks over at Daffy Duck and sees a mirage where Daffy's a roast duck rotating on a spit? That look.

To pin me, he had to hold my shoulders down on the mat for three seconds, when the ref would blow his whistle and give the mat that resounding *splaaat* slap. So that means I was guaranteed to last at least three seconds out there, and I loved the adrenaline of stepping out by myself, no teammates to lean on, the eyes of the crowd on me, maybe a dropped jaw or two, all the bitterly jealous guys on the other side of the room wishing they'd gained or lost a few pounds in time to pair off with me. I loved the squeaky noises of our wrestling shoes on the mat. I was a star, or at least part of the show, and I walked tall out there. Taking my stand. Defending my . . . *splaaat*!

On the way home, we bonded. If anyone resented me bringing our team record down, nobody ever mentioned it or made fun of me for it. We'd fought hard that day. Next year, some of us would make varsity; some of us would run around the gym waving a badminton racquet. But tonight, we sang the Stones all the way back to school.

Over two seasons, I lost fourteen matches. I made them earn it—no surrender, no retreat, no permanent spinal damage. I didn't count how many times I went the distance and lost on points, rather than getting pinned before the match ended, but I know there were a bunch of those. I learned a lot about bringing down an opponent and using his aggressive energy against him, as long as he doesn't have any muscles. If I ever end up in a bar brawl with a flamingo, I am taking that bastard down.

My wife still does not believe me.

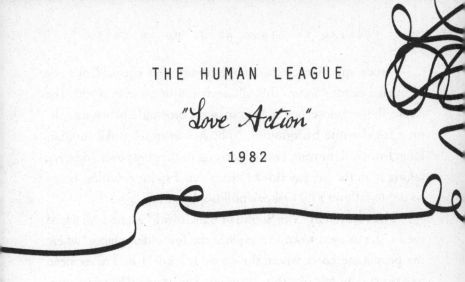

Around ninth grade, my trusty clock radio began playing something weird. First, it went *clink-clank*. Then it went *bloop-bloop*. After the *wrrrp-wrrrp* kicked in, there came a blizzard of *squisha-squisha-squisha* noises. It sounded like a Morse code transmission from another planet, a world of lust and danger and nonstop erotic cabaret. What *was* this? It was the twitchy, spastic, brand-new beat of synth-pop. For those of us who were "Kids in America" at the time, it was a totally divisive sound. You either loved it or hated it. My friends and I argued for hours over whether it even counted as rock and roll. I remember hearing a DJ explain that the Human League didn't have any instruments. No way—not even a drummer? Not even a *guitarist*? I was shocked.

I rode my bike to the public library and checked out the Human League's *Dare*. This album was a brave new world. The sleeve showed close-ups of their mascara eyes and lipstick mouths on a frigid white background. Nobody was smiling. All summer long, I worked mowing lawns, listening to that tape over and over, taking it on the subway ride to driver's ed. I spent countless hours trying to fathom Phil Oakey's philosophy of life.

I was moved by "The Sound of the Crowd," where Phil urged me to "get around town," to explore the forbidden places "where the people are good, where the music is loud." I had never been to a place remotely like this. It sounded awesome. The lyrics were a bit obscure, what with all the arcane cosmetics references ("The lines on a compact guide / A hat with alignment worn inside"— huh?), yet I devoured them. If I cracked his code well, I too would grow up to be a Phil Oakey, getting around the world on an existential quest for love action.

There were more where the League came from: Depeche Mode, Orchestral Manoeuvres in the Dark, Heaven 17, Duran Duran, Kim Wilde, my beloved Haysi Fantayzee. We got all the U.K. synth-poppers a year or so after the Brits were through with them, but we were glad to have them. Any arty Brit-twerp with a magenta wedge and octagonal drum pads was a go.

They were to the early '80s what girl groups like the Ronettes, the Shangri-Las, and the Chiffons were to the early '60s: queen pimps of teen bathos, pumping up the drums and the mascara to cosmic levels. All these nobodies teased up their hair to fire-hazard levels and dolled themselves up into glitter-encrusted sex cookies.

At the touch of a synth button, they turned into the things that dreams were made of.

The concept was New Romantic, which was a slippery term, since nobody ever admitted to being one. Even Duran Duran, who called themselves "New Romantics" in the first verse of their first single, didn't want to get stuck with a label this silly. New Romantic songs are questing through the world or elsewhere in search of pleasure and danger and beauty. No New Romantic songs were about sitting in your room and staring at the wallpaper, even though (as far as I could tell) that's probably how most New Romantic followers spent their time.

The New Romantics were a lot like the Old Romantics, the poets I was crazy about in high school—Shelley and Keats, Wordsworth and Blake—and none of those dead guys ever called themselves "Romantics" either. (Romanticism, like rockabilly or film noir, was a genre that only got its name after it was over.) John Keats declared, "What shocks the virtuous philosopher delights the camelion poet." Boy George sang about a "karma chameleon." Boy George and John Keats would have had a lot to say to each other—they were both poor London boys who dreamed up an extravagant mythology of transforming the world by transforming yourself. It was a sect where you had to commit to constant personal self-reinvention. That oldest of Romantics, William Blake, declared, "The tygers of wrath are wiser than the horses of instruction." And the New Romantics were most certainly tygers of wrath. They also obviously had a lot more fun than the Romantic poets, whose favorite recreational pastimes seemed to consist of catching tuberculosis, groping leech-gatherers and planting a deceased lover's head in a pot of basil.

The Human League were the ultimate New Romantics, at least in terms of how we heard them in America, and they won everyone over, crossing over to the pop charts in that incredibly pivotal year of 1982, the year of *Thriller* and *1999* and "Super Freak" and "I Love Rock N' Roll" and "I'm So Excited" and "Sexual Healing." Kiss-108, the disco station, was playing Yaz and the Human League; WCBN, the rock station, was playing Grandmaster Flash and Michael Jackson. The Human League fit right in to a world where the most exciting and adventurous music on the planet seemed to be exactly what was exploding on Top 40 radio. Yet they didn't lose their New Romantic cred by crossing over—quite the contrary. Their success validated the whole New Romantic credo.

The New Romantic anthem I studied most intently was "Love Action," where Phil sings, "This is Phil talking! I want to tell you what I've found out to be true!" I have to admit, I have loved the Human League passionately for years, and I have never totally figured out what Phil Oakey has found out to be true. But I've never stopped delving into the mystery.

I would have loved to have gone to the clubs that Phil was singing about, but I was in Milton, Massachusetts, and the only fan here was me. (Were there other Human League fans in town? How would I know? We weren't an outgoing bunch.)

I mean, it's one thing to decide you're Phil Oakey if you are Phil Oakey and you have that slide of hair down the side and the eyeliner. But it's pretty silly deciding you're a New Romantic when you're stranded in the suburbs mowing lawns, playing video games, translating Virgil and just in general being a miserable little teenage fuck. At a thrift store in Saugus, I paid six dollars for a jacket that I hoped looked like the one Phil Oakey wears in the "Love Action" video, but when I got it home, it looked suspiciously like a shoulder-pad maitre d' jacket left in the Dumpster behind Mr. Tux. I'm sure the collar was real velvet, though. (Pretty sure. Velvet's fuzzy, right?)

Wearing this jacket to play Asteroids at the South Shore Plaza did not make me feel like a glamorous man of the world. It made me feel somewhat of a tool. But then, Phil had warned me that suffering was part of this path. And I knew ridicule is nothing to be scared of.

My sisters took me shopping and I came home with pants with pleats, which ended badly. (I blame a certain Scritti Politti video. What can I say? I was more into fashion theory than practice.) Although I worshipped Bowie, Roxy and the dashing New Romantics they left behind in their wake like so many droplets of champagne-flavored sweat, and studied their sartorial elegance, I was doomed to dress more like the harmonica player for the J. Geils Band. But I had the devotion, which was much more important than a genuine wedge haircut.

If I *had* wanted a wedge haircut, I have no idea how I'd have gotten one. Like everyone else in town, I went to the only barber around, Singin' Jack in East Milton Square. Jack gave everyone the same haircut, while singing along with the radio's Continuous Lite Favorites. He was particularly into Jim Croce, and you were lucky to show up for your haircut on a Croce day, because you would get to hear him sing "I'll Have to Say I Love You in a Song" as he snipped. (Kenny Rogers days were unlucky, and if Jack was singing "Ruby, Don't Take Your Love to Town," it was best to sneak out before you ended up with a whiffle.) Since Jack was erratic at best, it would be foolhardy to ask him to try anything sideways, or to bring in a *Dare* tape for inspiration.

It didn't matter. New wave wasn't really about the right look; it was a state of mind. Still, shame about those pleats.

Something about this style of pop lent itself to devotion from shut-ins, losers, social twitchers like me. The electro bleeps were whispers from the wider world outside, beckoning us out, like the lights flickering from the stereo. I would watch the red vertical flickers of the EQ and imagine they were skyscrapers of a city just outside my window, a city full of the kind of clubs where the clubsters were getting around town in the sort of clubs Phil Oakey would sing about, and occasionally recruit girl singers from, and dance freely without worrying about startling the nice old lady next door. It was a club you could join just by believing it existed.

In any new-wave fan mag, you could find the lonely-hearts pen-pal section. From the *Smash Hits* from February 1983, which I've always kept because it had Kajagoogoo on the cover:

> "I'm a 15-year-old girl looking for any Boy George Looka-likes or anyone else interested in Culture Club. If you're 15+ and dress weird write to Girl George, Essex."

"Mad, blonde Swedish girl, 17, wants strange friends from London into Bowie, Toyah, Adam til 81, punks and pretty boys. Milla, Sweden."

"I'm lonely. My name's Warren, I'm 15 and desperate to hear from any females into Coronation St, Blancmange and Motorhead. My CB handle is Pigpen."

Still using CB radio in 1983? Poor guy. But these were the fans that flocked to the League. These were my people.

With new wave for inspiration, I took to the stage, playing Duncan in the tenth grade production of *Macbeth*. (If you're not familiar with the play, Macbeth kills Duncan to possess his donuts. He ends up having to kill Banquo for a coffee.) The kid who played Macbeth was the son of Franklin Cover, the late great TV actor who played Tom Willis on *The Jeffersons*, so I can look back on my acting career secure in the knowledge that Tom Willis has seen my Duncan.

"Don't You Want Me" was the huge hit, a song that brought in the rock crowd, the gold-chained disco crowd, the Top 40 stations, everybody. It was massively influential on the club music that went on to dominate the decade. (Madonna's first hit, "Burning Up," nicked the drum track from the League's "The Sound of the Crowd.") Afrika Bambaataa once said, "I remember when we all heard 'Don't You Want Me Baby' and people would say, 'That's all synthesizers, that's a drum machine,' and we'd say, 'It can't be, those sound like real drums.'"

They'd started out as all-male arty techno introverts from the northern steeltown Sheffield, which was full of great (and mostly incredibly solemn) synth groups, as chronicled in the fantastic documentary *Made in Sheffield*. They began their climb with "Being Boiled," an art-twaddle track that began with the lines "Listen to the voice of Buddha / Saying stop your sericulture," and then proceeded to get silly. (In case you're wondering, "sericulture" means farming silk from worms and has nothing to do with Buddha.) But the silliness was lovable—they were all too human, this League.

The inspiring thing about *Dare* was the emotional journey behind it, the fact that they got there after starting out with "Being Boiled." They began as an art band for boys, and then became a pop group for girls. If these guys could go from being dour, introspective twits who not only met girls but had girls *in the group*, well, there was hope for all of us, right?

Why did they let the girls sing in the first place? When I interviewed Phil Oakey a few years ago, he told me, "We'd made two LPs as a male-only group. But two of the guys left and we had to do a tour, so we went out and recruited a couple of women. And then we had to give them something to do, really." After the other guys in the group left to form Heaven 17, Phil was out at a local club, the excellently named Crazy Daisy Disco, and picked up a couple of girls. They crossed the line from fans to starlets. As one of those girls, Suzanne, put it in 1981, "He wanted a tall black singer and he got two short white girls who couldn't sing."

But they had personality, the totally ordinary charm that put the human in the league. Together they bumbled into pop stardom, without paying any dues. In the U.K., the band was thoughtful enough to release their singles with color codes on the label; the red ones were for "poseurs" and the blue ones for "ABBA fans," but anyone who liked the League could be both a poseur and an ABBA fan.

I guess the League fascinated me because they truly embodied the anyone-can-do-it spirit of this music—in fact, the hardly-anyone-*can't*-do-it spirit. Phil cheerfully admitted to the fan mags that he only started singing in the first place because he failed at playing the synthesizer. At a time when guitar bands complained that keyboard geeks were too lazy to learn a real instrument, Phil Oakey had the gall to announce he found synths just *too hard to play*.

Oh, how I pondered the Phil Oakey perspective on life. The hours I spent poring over the lyrics, wondering how he did what he did. He seemed to have provocative ideas about love and religion. "The Things That Dreams Are Made Of" articulated his worldview: "Everybody needs love and adventure / Everybody needs two or three friends."

From the sounds of this album, Phil Oakey spent most of his evenings in glitzy clubs arguing with girls about philosophy. Life was a battle of Good Times versus Hard Times, every man for himself, God against all. He sang like a Sinatra-style cocktail crooner, sharing some of the hard truths he'd learned along the way, alluding to broken marriages and dashed dreams. "I've lain awake and cried at night over what love made me do," he sang, and I couldn't help but be jealous, less for the love part than the glamour of having tragic love affairs to look back upon with rue.

I yearned to cultivate decadence, without the hard work of actually doing anything decadent. The seductivosity of this music went without saying. Phil Oakey was a sensuous man, and took his stand as such. Indeed, he came on like an even more pretentious Barry White (his next project after *Dare* was a remix album under the name of the League Unlimited Orchestra) and, supposedly, putting on "Open Your Heart" in the right bedroom would lead to existential crises with sexual resolutions. In the "Love Action" video, Phil gets taken hostage by agents who strap him to a chair and interrogate him. They apparently represent the pro-hate faction. But Phil defiantly tells them, "No matter what you put me through, I'll still believe in love," a very Morrissey thing to say, although not even Morrissey would have the gall to put it this way. And like Morrissey, Phil specialized in feeding me ludicrously unusable advice about how to conduct an adult emotional life. For him, being a New Romantic was more than a fashion fad—it was a code of honor, an ethic.

My fantasy life, warped completely by the Human League, began to resemble a Human League song. I would judge everything by whether it was new wave or not. I related to Johnny Slash on the show *Square Pegs*; any time one of the other kids would call him punk, Johnny would pull his shades down and say, "Not punk, new wave. Totally different head, man! Totally different head!" Or as John Keats would say, "I see, and sing, by my own eyes inspir'd."

ORCHESTRAL MANOEUVRES
IN THE DARK

"Enola Gay"

1982

Spain was where I learned to dance with girls. Not dance with a girl, but in a gang of girls. This was a discovery that shook my foundations. I was used to school dances, where the boys stood on one side, the girls on the other, and you awkwardly asked a girl to dance. Maybe. But just going out on the floor with a bunch of girls and dancing? You could do this? It was like I'd discovered some secret crack in the fabric of the universe, something not just new but previously unthinkable. It was like I found the Shroud of Turin in my sock drawer.

I spent the summer of '82 in a student exchange program at Colegio Estudio, a school in Madrid. The Spanish girls were all groovy. They all listened to Simon & Garfunkel, who they called

"See-MOAN y Gar-FOON-kel." They all listened to "techno-pop," music that in my country only weirdos liked. They wore *minifaldas* on hot days. They had very strong feelings about the evils of the Catholic Church, unless they actually had Catholic mothers, in which case I wasn't allowed near them in the first place. I fell in love with every single one of them.

I'm not sure how Angela and Nuria became my friends. My third or fourth day, I was sitting by myself at lunch. Angela and Nuria came up and said, You're eating with us. *Con nosotras.* I said okay. Angela had a mod bob and a high-pitched voice that chattered constantly. She gave me a book of poems by Antonio Machado, her favorite. Nuria didn't talk as much as Angela; in fact, she barely said a word all summer. I thought Angela looked a bit like a pigeon, which I meant as a compliment, but I knew better than to say it out loud, even though the Spanish word for "pigeon" is the same as "dove."

We spent the summer going to *discotecas* and dancing—two Spanish girls, two American girls we knew, and me. Angela, Nuria, Kate and Ligia would primp and change outfits and put on their makeup, then we'd ride the subway, sometimes with other Spanish girls like Cristina or Casilda. We all kissed one another on the cheek twice a night, hello and good-bye. Lust was in the air, all of it mine, but somehow these girls knew I was never going to make a move on them. I wish I know how they could tell. Yes, I was in another country, speaking another language, but I still had the Esperanto word for "non-ass-grabber" written on my forehead. It was the most demanding social life I'd ever had; escorting these girls was constant work. My role was unclear to me, but it was obviously a good gig to have.

One of them once made out with a guy while dancing, then claimed he was no good at all. That's the only time I ever saw any of them get romantic on the floor. They weren't here to mingle; they were here to dance and show off. As I got older, I learned that my role is usually served by hot gay dudes who don't know they're gay yet, rather than straight boys who are merely shy, so I don't know how I got so lucky. Weren't there any bona fide gay dudes around? Guess not.

The perks of being in this gang were massive. It was my introduction to nightlife, to clubbing, the thrill of *discoteca* culture. I remember the flashing lights of the Metro, as if we were already in the disco just by heading out there. The ecstatic tingle of anticipation, almost unbearable, as each station passed by. The girls all nervous in their *minifaldas*. The metallic glint of the elevator, riding up from the Metro stop, knowing what was up there waiting. The billboards on the block *("Martini: Te Invita a Vivir")* that served as signposts to remind us we were on our way. The boys outside on their Motovespa scooters. Walking up to the door, with that adrenaline rush of fear. Maybe something will go wrong? What if they won't let us in? A private party? That happens. But we always got in, maybe because we just had one boy and a gaggle of chicas.

Pacha, that was the place. We were all sixteen—that was the age to get in. It was one thousand pesetas, about ten bucks, on weekends, but only seven hundred on weeknights. One final split-second wave of fear as you paid the money at the window. The pale green ticket stub. Getting in. The air-conditioning hitting you like a full-body slam. Crowding on the floor, the girls using their stiletto elbows, working our way across the room, somewhere near the corner. Finding our spot. *There*. We're in.

The girls started dancing, their skirts spinning away, and I followed along. The music was a barrage of insanely sexy techno-pop songs I'd never heard before—Depeche Mode's "Just Can't Get Enough," Haircut 100's "Favourite Shirts," Orchestral Manoeuvres in the Dark's "Enola Gay." And the Human League—dancing to that, with actual girls. Can't think, I'll pass out. Just keep going. What is this sound? Who knows? Up! Down! Turn around! Please don't let me hit the ground!

At school dances back home, I'd felt awkward and conspicuous, but here the lights were out and nobody could see me except my gang. The other dudes ogled my friends. They danced up to the girls' faces and spoke to the American girls in English, saying, "I am your boyfriend" or "I am fast, I am good." They danced up to the Spanish girls and sang the lyrics of whatever song was playing, usually in English. The girls would hold my hand and the boys would go away. Then they would let go of my hand. Most nights I was the only boy any of them would talk to. On the floor, I was one of the girls, twirling as one of the ladies of the night.

None of us ever drank, despite the fact that we were all of legal drinking age and there was a bar. This seems a bit remarkable in retrospect, but it was never even an issue. Why waste *discoteca* time? At some point during the night, Pacha always shut off the music for a half hour or so, so they could host an urban-cowboy contest on a mechanical leather bull. We stood around, stomping our shoes with impatience, watching the clientele hop on the bull and tumble off, while the sound system blasted country music. Then the techno-pop came on again.

Some nights, we stayed home to watch *Dallas*. They were two seasons behind the United States, so I ruined the show for them by revealing everything that was going to happen to Pam Ewing. I promised not to tell anyone else, so Angela could ruin it for the whole school.

Sometimes they trusted me to pick the evening's entertainment. I took them to see *The Graduate* (*El graduado*), telling them it had lots of Simon & Garfunkel. But I squandered my credibility dragging them to *Airplane!* retitled *Aterrizza como puedas*, or "Land However You Can." I assured them that in America, this was universally recognized as the funniest movie ever made. How I laughed, the lone hyena in the theater, at all the badly dubbed Spanish versions of jokes I knew by heart. The girls failed to see the humor of *"Yo hablo jive"* or *"No me llamas Shirley."*

I tried explaining why it was funny. See, in *ingles*, the word *"seguramente"* is "surely," which sounds like *el nombre de una persona.* Shirley! *¿Divertido, no?*

I was never allowed to pick the movie again. To punish me, they took me to *Midnight Express*, about an American boy who gets thrown into a foreign jail because he tries to smuggle drugs. The movie was torture to watch, although it did introduce me to the concept of bras that unhook in the front.

These were the coolest girls I'd ever met. They called the

Smurfs *"Pitufos."* They argued over politics and corrected my grammar. They took me to juice bars, and whenever the radio would play Depeche Mode or Soft Cell, they'd yell *"¡Ponelo mas alto!"* We gave one another profanity lessons in our native tongues. They took me shopping, where I learned the joys of spending warm summer days indoors, waiting for hours outside changing rooms and repeating "that one also looks very nice" in Spanish. They were teaching me a whole new language, in more ways than one.

Surely there were girls like this back home? Surely not. And *no me llamas Shirley!*

Sometimes we listened to records. Yet even though they went out clubbing two or three nights a week, they did not own any techno-pop records. They collected the acoustic folkies like Bob Dylan and Victor Jara, who I'd heard of because the Clash liked him; he'd been killed by the fascists in Chile for singing songs about girls who were killed by the fascists in Spain. I liked listening to records with these girls so much, I even drove myself, by sheer force of will, to enjoy Simon & Garfunkel, and began relating to their sensitive little folk songs. *Hello doucheness, my old friend. I've come to suck with you again.*

They talked about the Spanish Civil War like it was yesterday, and everybody at school had very complex political opinions. The little brother of my Spanish host family spray-painted an *A* in a circle on the wall of the garage, which (as he explained) meant he was an anarchist. If you wore a Spanish flag on the wristband of your watch, it meant you were a fascist. I had never met real-life fascists or anarchists or socialists. I was used to calling someone "fascist" when they borrowed my pencil without resharpening it, so I was shocked to hear people call themselves fascists. There had been an attempted military coup three months earlier, and everybody had fierce ideas about that. The school had a mural of Guernica up in the lobby, but it was covered with a glass panel to keep right-wing students from defacing it with graffiti.

There were fascist discos and socialist discos. One of our Spanish classmates invited us to a party at a place called Aguacates. Kate, Ligia and I never refused a chance to go clubbing, but the Spanish girls wouldn't go, because they said it was the right-wing disco. I was like, who cares, it's just disco, right? At midnight the DJ played *Arriba España,"* the perky theme song of the Fuerza Nueva Party, and everybody rushed to the floor to sing along and gave fascist salutes, even the very drunk girl in the fuchsia tube top whose cleavage I had spent the evening admiring. I remember you, Amanda, and even though I appreciated how the salute made your right breast stretch a little farther out of your top, I didn't care anymore. I even stopped wondering if your bra was the kind that unhooked in the front.

We left Aguacates a little rattled. I understood why my friends wouldn't go there. It was like "The National Front Disco," one of my favorite Morrissey songs, about how there's a group of friends and one of them starts going to the fascist disco and everybody grieves because they've lost their boy. In general, political enemies did not party together.

All summer long, the songs were the only souvenir from the night I could hold on to the next day—remembering all those sensations was overwhelming in sunlight, so I would hum the tunes to myself. I had to learn them by heart, because I had no way of finding out who sang them or how to get a copy. I knew I'd never hear them again back home. Most of them didn't exist in the United States yet, and many wouldn't get any airplay until the 1990s, when they became staples of '80s-at-eight radio shows. Mecano were easily the most popular group in the *discotecas*— they were local heroes, a Madrid trio with two smoldering synth boys and a pretty girl in a pouffy dress. The boys played keyboards, or as they were called on the album cover, "*teclados*," which meant "touched things" and therefore seemed sexual by definition. The boys always frowned and looked mean in pictures; the girl singer, Ana Torroja, looked like she despised the boys. Hot!

Whenever I looked at the picture, I imagined how great it would be to join this group. What was Ana Torroja really like? Was one of the boys in the group her boyfriend? Or were the boys a couple? All their songs were either about putting on makeup or going to parties. Their big hit, "*Me Colé en una Fiesta*," was about both—Ana crashes a party where she isn't invited, sees her boyfriend dance with another girl, and cries all the way home. I had already heard plenty of songs with this story, but this one I was actually dancing to, which made it all completely different.

The boy in my Spanish host family, Jorge Luis, was into metal and punk. The only male friends I made in Spain were his friends, so we sat in their rooms listening to Iron Maiden. They made me translate "The Number of the Beast" for them. *("¡Seis! ¡Seis! ¡Seis!")* They thought guys who went to *discotecas* were not so cool. The kids at school brought more records for me to translate—nobody in the United States even remembered Meat Loaf, but these kids loved all the Meat Loaf records and (incredibly) Jim Steinman's solo album. In gratitude, Jorge Luis presented me with an essay collection by Che Guevara, apparently because I still had a few unticked boxes on my Eighties Teen Cliché Bingo card.

I could see why music was a serious business here. This was a place where every detail of your identity—politics, religion, fashion—seemed to hang on your taste in pop. If you liked a certain kind of music, you dressed the part every day. The gap between Iron Maiden and Depeche Mode was as deep as the gap between anarchists and fascists. Unfortunately, the only Catholic kids I met were fascists, so I went to church by myself, where I seemed to be the only person under a hundred. I was afraid I'd crush someone's wrist in the sign of peace.

The city was full of subcultures I'd only read about in new-wave magazines. Casilda took me roller-skating with her boyfriend, who was a mod. A real-life mod! He had the long parka with the Jam's logo painted on back, and drainpipe trousers. We went to the park, where we sat on the grass so he could glare at the rockers, who sported leather jackets and rockabilly hair, just like in the movies. I could not believe I was watching actual mods and rockers; it was like I had died and gone to music boy heaven.

The weeks went by. Eventually, I was going home. I was never gonna dance again. *Con nosotras*—I was going to miss that. In America, I'd go right back to being who I was before, a fate so awful I could barely imagine it. I tried to start conversations with the girls about all the good times we were having—I hoped someone would take the hint to explain what it all meant, and how I could make it happen again back home. Where I was never going to get into a disco, or hear "Da Da Da," or eat gazpacho, even though I didn't even like gazpacho. I tried to make them nostalgic for our crazy summer before it was even over, slipping *Airplane!* jokes into the conversation.

"You've got to take me to the hospital."

"*¿Que es?*"

"*Es un edificio lleno de infirmadades.*"

Like the airplane in the movie, I was going to have to come down sometime. The landing would be bumpy. *Aterriza como puedas*—land however you can.

The night before I left, we went to a house party where the hostess kept spinning "Enola Gay," a song about two kids wanting to make out so bad it's like a bomb about to go off. When their lips meet, it's a nuclear explosion that blows up the whole world, and nothing will ever be the same. It didn't sound like an exaggeration. I got sad kissing Angela and Nuria good-bye, which made me feel like an idiot, so I confessed that I felt *embarazado.* They giggled. I had just told them I was pregnant. I never saw them again.

I cradled my head in my hands the whole flight home. The next day, my mom took me and my little sister to the South Shore Plaza to see *E.T.* It had been a huge hit for weeks, but Caroline had waited until I came home so she could see it with me. She must've been the only six-year-old in America who would make a sacrifice like that for her jet-lagged big brother. The Saturday afternoon matinee was full of little kids, their parents and exactly one sixteen-year-old boy. It was basically a movie about a sad Muppet who thought he was David Bowie. Caroline broke down sometime during the opening credits. I put my arm around her and kept it there as she wept through the movie. The dialogue was all in English, yet drowned out by sobs, wails, chokes and snarfles. Everybody around me needed a tissue and nobody had one. Like *E.T.*, I was home.

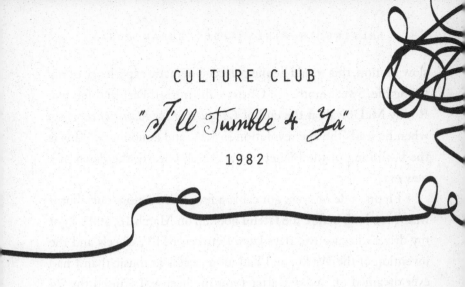

MTV was, roughly speaking, the greatest thing ever. Everything changed when MTV came to town. All of a sudden, it was like "awesome" was a verb, and we were conjugating it all night long. I awesome, you awesome, he, she, it awesome! We awesome! They awesome! Okay, let's do the Spanish second-person plural familiar: *Vosotros awesome!*

The first time I bit into the M-apple was at my buddy Flynn's house, where we trouped after school the day he got cable. The first video we caught was the Psychedelic Furs' "Pretty in Pink." Hey, there's a rock star walking across a checkerboard floor! Which gets reflected in his wraparound shades. And a mysterious yet alluring lady in a red miniskirt. If only we got to see a mirror shattering in slow motion, this would be the perfect cinematic experience of my young life. Sweet mother of Christ—the mirror! Perfect. I felt like Roddy McDowall at the end of *Conquest of the Planet of the Apes*, when he leads the ape revolution in L.A. and announces, "This is the beginning of the Planet of the Apes!" Clearly, the dawn of a new era.

Flynn's side of town got cable a few weeks before ours, but it wasn't too long before the fateful hookup on March 16, 1983. I got my driver's license two days later. Between MTV, wheels and the invention of the Walkman, I had more access to music than I had ever dreamed of. The day after I got my license, I cruised the '74 Chevy Nova into Boston to go drive around with my buddy Terry just so we could play the radio. Okay, it was just an AM radio, no windshield wipers, no heater and a backseat floor that was completely rotted through. It was a car that had seen better days and crashed into most of them. My mom used to drive this car into the inner-city public school where she taught fourth grade. It still had little dings from all the rocks thrown at it. Her students were so appalled by Mrs. Sheffield's car, they offered to steal her a Lincoln (much easier to steal than a Mercedes) as this car reflected badly on them. Hey, who cared? At least the *radio* worked.

But the combination of wheels and MTV exploded my musical universe. One Friday night, I drove to the dance in the high school gym, drove back home to watch the world premiere of Michael Jackson's "Beat It" video at ten, and then drove back to the dance so I could tell everyone how awesome it was and make my first pitiful attempts to copy that dance at the end.

On MTV, with the world watching, rock stars invented whole new ways to blow fortunes they didn't have on fire-hazard hair, spandex pants, octagonal synth-drums, keytars, supermodels humping the hoods of foreign cars, and other garishly bad ideas. It was a night town world of bossy girls and swirly boys, animated by computer disco bleeps and the whiff of hair dye and one another's pheromones. These babes had some battle scars, but they flaunted their scars and called them baubles. Boy George felt self-conscious about his wide hips, so he wore dresses that made it impossible not to notice them, and shook them back and forth, back and forth, turning them into an ornament for his inherent gorgeousness. They put on slap by the shovel-load and wore way too much face for any person's face to hold.

They knew pop glamour isn't something you earn by the rules, it's something you steal and cheat and lie for, so a star like Boy George didn't have to be conventionally handsome, or conventionally anything. They did evil deeds to get famous, did even more evil deeds to stay there, made their deals with the pop devils. No other genre would have wanted them, but new wave had to take them in because it was the island of misfit toys, with funny-looking people who decided to be gorgeous and boring-looking people who decided to be funny-looking. All these new-wave fashion tarts, all these radar lovers and data pimps and glitter-encrusted sex cookies crept out of my radio and took over my world, breaking on through to the other peroxide and feasting on the virgin sacrifice of my body and soul.

It was all just teenage code for pretending to be somebody

else, which is how I spent 99 percent of my waking hours, like any teenager. I would hear a Bananarama song and I would wish there were three of me so I could paint the letters *W O W* on my three asses and then bend over and do the Bananarama dances all day.

MTV had twenty-four hours a day to fill, and they didn't have enough normal music to play, so they were forced to pad it out with all sorts of abnormal music. So when you tuned in to MTV, you didn't just see normal music with pictures. Instead you saw there were lots of musicians out there who didn't buy into the '80s rock-radio consensus that rock was heavy metal and everything else was disco. You saw how they moved, how they posed, what they thought was cool. You found out what their names were, and what their latest albums were called. Maybe you were hooked, maybe you weren't—there'd be another video on in a minute.

No doubt, MTV would have rather been playing normal rock, i.e., metal, all along. It certainly played the hell out of Zebra, Triumph and every other dodgy metal act that could be coaxed in front of a camera. But with so much airtime to fill and so little product to plug in, it was forced to play these clowns. And along the way, MTV did something it never planned on doing and most likely never wanted to do—it created a whole new audience. Because lots of us saw these new-wave bands and thought they were the greatest thing we'd ever fucking heard.

Teenage boys love to argue about things. It doesn't even matter about what—we would argue about baseball, books, politics, whether *Scarface* was the greatest movie of all time or whether that honor belonged to *Vice Squad*. Without MTV to argue about,

I'm sure we would have found some other topic to hash out over our meat loaf sandwiches. Who knows—maybe we even would have sat at a table where some girls were sitting. But with MTV exposing everyone to hours and hours of otherwise unavailable music, girls would just have to wait, because there was arguing to be done.

And since teenage boys love to argue about silly shit, my entire high school lunchroom became a daily debate over what was new wave and what wasn't. Were ZZ Top new wave? Was Billy Idol new wave? Were the Clash punk or new wave? Was Spandau Ballet rock or pop? Was there a case to be made for Duran Duran? Needless to say, Duran Duran inspired the most venomous arguments. But there was always new shit to fight over, because MTV was always blasting new shit.

And all these new rock stars were battling it out for my soul. Joe Strummer (my hero) urged me to fight war and intolerance. Prince (the Joe Strummer of orgasms) urged me to join his sexual revolution. Men Without Hats warned me that friends who don't dance are no friends at all. Cyndi Lauper advised me to find a bunch of cool girls and follow them around and do whatever they told me to do, because girls just want to have fun and boys without girls are no fun at all. This was a lot of Weltanschauung for one little altar boy to take in.

It can be hard to tell if a song is new wave or not. The debate got pretty intense in certain rarefied circles, e.g., Flynn's mom's basement. These debates still rage in the overstuffed and underoccupied crania of those who hold new wave dear. There are, however, a few telltale signs. If it's a song about shoes, pants or hair, it's new wave. If they have a funny name, it's new wave. If the singer is German, it's new wave, unless it's the Scorpions. If you think the singer is German, but he's really not, then that's an extraordinarily rarefied level of new wave, and probably means a kind of new-wave satori has been reached. For some reason I assumed Peter Godwin was German because of "Images of Heaven." He sounded totally German, especially because he was pining over a girlfriend who didn't exist. (Songs about girls who don't exist? Very new wave.)

I felt vaguely betrayed when I found out Peter Godwin was English, but he also wrote one of my favorite songs on David Bowie's *Let's Dance*, "Criminal World." When you successfully fake being German, and Bowie sings one of your songs, you are probably one of the six or seven most new-wave people on the planet.

If you have a song about nuclear war, you are new wave. If you sing about gay sex and nuclear war, you are Frankie Goes to Hollywood. If you are a hot German chick and you sing about nuclear war, you are Nena. If you sang about starting a nuclear war via making out, you are Orchestral Manoeuvres in the Dark. If you sing about nuclear war *and* girlfriends who don't exist, you are scoring some serious new-wave points. (Why are you trying so hard, anyway? You must be Orchestral Manoeuvres in the Dark again!) If you start to sing the word "ass" but change your mind and substitute a drum solo, you are Huey Lewis, which is as far from new wave as you can get.

Sure, all this new wave was pretty silly. Did we care? Nope.

We liked it that way. "One cheap illusion could still be divine," Peter Godwin sang in "Images of Heaven," and by that theological reasoning, new wave was truly the church of the poison mind.

The elements of a cool video were far more simple: first, you needed a cool song, because if you were Tom Petty, it did not matter how much money you spent on your video, you were always just going to be Tom Petty. A hot girl in the video helped as well. But locations were really important. Guitar heroes had always aimed to sound like they were playing their guitar solos on a mountaintop. Now, you actually could stand on a literal mountaintop, wind whipping in your hair, and play that solo, even if you were the guy from Tears for Fears.

Now that you could play on a mountaintop, or some other stupid place, you didn't really have an excuse not to, right? Echo & the Bunnymen did their guitar solo on top of a glacier. U2 played their guitars on a mountain in a blizzard. You could play on the beach in Sri Lanka (Duran Duran) or on a desert plain at sunset, like David Bowie in "Let's Dance," miming to a guitar solo that was actually played by Stevie Ray Vaughan. David Lee Roth climbed a mountain, but forgot to bring a guitar. Culture Club did "Karma Chameleon" on a Mississippi River steamboat. Their video had a plot. Plots were not very cool. But Boy George's fingerless gloves? Cool.

Laurie Anderson complained that MTV was all "boys playing guitar in the shower, boys playing guitar on the roof." But both of those ideas were fairly excellent. Dave Edmunds had a breakthrough with his "Information" video, playing his guitar solo while standing at the urinal. I guess someone had to try it. Bryan Adams was, I believe, the first to attempt rocking out in an empty swimming pool. Aaaaaaand the last.

There was an intense debate in our cafeteria over who would be the first rock star to make a video where he got crucified and sing his latest hit from up on the cross. Flynn thought it would be Ozzy. I argued for Billy Idol. We were both right: it was Def Leppard, in "Bringin' on the Heartbreak." (And Joe Elliott had the gall to get himself crucified on a boat, which Rick Allen seemed to be paddling down the River Styx. These dudes left nothing to chance, did they?)

If I'm not mistaken, the all-time standard in the "location, location, location" wars was set by Journey in "Separate Ways," the one where they went to the lumberyard. Steve Perry sang about his broken heart while clambering over a stack of two-by-fours. Journey walked around the lumberyard feeling sad about their lady love, who (naturally) was right there in the lumberyard, strutting around in her leather miniskirt. How exactly did this girl end up there? Was she looking for her friends? Did they play a prank on her, calling to say, "Yo, Maureen, we'll all meet up after school at the mall . . . I mean, Curly's Lumberyard, over by the dock. No, rilly. Lumber's hot. Wear those cute earrings!"

But the absolute absurdity of the surroundings just made the song better, proving beyond doubt that Steve Perry has no shame as he wails the lines, "We're caught between confusion and pain! Paaaa-yeeeeen! PAIN!" Who knows, maybe Journey really just liked to go pace around the lumberyard when they needed to sort some shit out. I hope the carpentry community returned their love.

Thanks to MTV, the new-wave virus spread everywhere. Anybody could make a new-wave record, and everybody did when it looked like there was some money in it. I mean, Joe Walsh made a new-wave record. Herbie Hancock made a new-wave record. So did Van Halen, Phil Collins, the Bee Gees, the Who, the Stones, Donna Summer, Neil Young, the Grateful Dead, everybody. Hell, even Dean Martin gave it a go with "Since I Met You Baby." In 1982, when a whole year went by without a new Police album, everybody tried making fake Police records, from Robert Plant to Rush.

As a new-wave aficionado, I thought that for most of these guys, their new-wave sellout record was the greatest thing they'd ever done. Gino Vannelli, a Vegas lounge singer, made the unbelievably great "Black Cars." Billy Joel had a number one hit with "It's Still Rock and Roll to Me," which inspired Weird Al Yankovic to make fun of him in "It's Still Billy Joel to Me": "Now everybody thinks new wave is super / Just ask Linda Ronstadt or even Alice Cooper." Linda Ronstadt's new-wave song, "How Do I Make You," was pretty lame. But Alice Cooper's "Clones (We're All)" was really great!

MTV dreams made their way into my head for keeps. When I imagine the afterlife, I picture it as the Eurythmics' video "Who's That Girl?" A tacky club, a red carpet, lots of half-famous people jostling around. You look and say, hey, there's somebody I remember. Boy George? Flash! Hey, isn't that Bananarama? Flash!

Please, boys, no more photos. Flash! Kajagoogoo, right? I know that dude! Everybody's there. You make chitchat with random scenester faces, waiting your turn for the ones you really want to talk to. That's okay. No pressure. Because as soon as the song is over, there will be another one, and in an hour or two, MTV will play this video again. All the same people will be there, over and over, all night long to the break of dawn.

I used to wait for hours for MTV to show this video. MTV and insomnia naturally went together, maybe because so many of the songs and videos were inspired by the kind of insomnia induced by pills and powders. So it felt natural to watch till dawn, hoping to get just one more look, one more moment with those faces. But now it's always there on YouTube, like everything else from the vaults of music-video history. There's no special occasion, no ceremony, but I click replay anyway. It's always on.

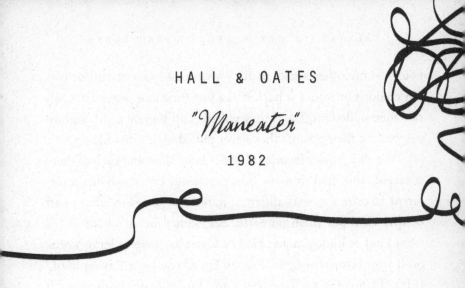

Is there a word in the language more beautiful than "Oates"? Say it loud, and his music is playing. Say it soft and it's almost like praying.

Oates. John Oates. You could argue the 1980s officially ended the day he shaved the mustache in 1991, but the mustache is still the Oatestache, and he made it America's stache for a long and honorable run. It has been argued in some quarters that Hall held him back, but I would not say that is true. I would say, "Oates."

One of the many fascinating things about the most successful boy-boy duo in the history of showbiz is that they are, as far as I can tell, the only act in history that became new wave. There were lots of classic rock guys who tried to make new-wave records and failed. Many other artists made a great new-wave record or two, but couldn't or wouldn't hack it as a full-time new-wave act. Only two men pulled it off, and they pulled it off together, although (if you believe their claims) they never pulled each other off.

We all have our favorite Hall & Oates jams, and each of them is sacred. They had so many hits, practically everybody has a different favorite for every different mood and occasion. That's part of why God put them on earth. See, sometimes it's hard to tell what kind of idiot you are. Hall & Oates are here to let us know. So if your favorite song is "Private Eyes," you are a "raving idiot." If it's "I Can't Go for That (No Can Do)," you are "blithering." If it's "Method of Modern Love," you are "savant."

I am a "hopeless idiot," and ergo my favorite Hall & Oates song is "Maneater," except on those special occasions when I prefer "Did It in a Minute," which shifts my idiot profile to "village."

"Kiss on My List" was the first time Hall & Oates made a new-wave hit, but it was "You Make My Dreams" that made them a bona fide new-wave group. They went all-out in that direction, leaving their folkie '70s adult soft-rock incarnation behind. They'd already been around forever—I remember that when they put out their album *Along the Red Ledge*, there was a radio ad proclaiming, "It's like hearing Daryl and John for the first time!" Yet they gambled their history on a dizzy, bouncy synth sound that must have seemed like a fad at the time. They didn't just go for the new-wave novelty hit—they threw all their non–new-wave baggage aside. They got the haircuts, the suits, the silly pants, and rolled all the way with it, and (of course) got a lot more popular than they'd ever been before. They were not just carpetbaggers. We loved them for trying so hard and for caring enough to get the details right. They had a lot to lose, and no reason to expect that we would embrace them, but (if I may speak for the new-wave-dork-circa-1982 community for a moment) we did. They were the only superstars who got the new-wave pass.

They embraced us right back, churning their "Kiss on My List" profits back into a new wardrobe of brighter, baggier pants. The only other previously popular band I can think of that went new wave and got away with it was the J. Geils Band, but I have to disqualify them a bit, because (1) I'm from Boston, so I overrate this band so wildly I tend to give them credit for things they never achieved, so I have to take even my own crazed enthusiasm with a grain of salt, (2) they were slightly better at being rock than being new wave, and (3) they broke up right after they went new wave, at the height of their *Freeze-Frame* fame, which meant they never got a chance to make their "Maneater," although they came close with "Flamethrower."

"Maneater" is from the album H_2O, which has Hall & Oates' second-gayest album cover. Since gay was nothing but a compliment in the new-wave book in 1982, there was nothing not to praise about an album with a cover that showed two men perspiring as they stared into each other's eyes, one on one as it were. They were probably not having sex out of camera range when they took this photo, but you could have fooled any of us. Daryl Hall actually had to explain in *Rolling Stone* that he was not into Oates that way ("he's not my type—too short and dark"); he added, "The idea of sex with a man doesn't turn me off," which was a pretty freaking badass thing for a mainstream pop star to say in the '80s. (Boy George never came out and said anything like that—but then, he didn't really have to, did he?) Naif that I was, I remember reading this and saying, "Wait, that doesn't mean he's actually had premarital sex, does it?" That's right—I was sixteen years old, and still believed that Hall & Oates were virgins. They sure liked each other a lot, though, and we liked them to like each other.

I first heard this album at my friend Terry's house, where we listened to it over and over one rainy Saturday afternoon as we played Stratego. We had spent the previous hours of the afternoon listening to the Clash's *Sandinista!* and the Psychedelic Furs' *Talk Talk Talk*, so we felt pretty daring and open-minded for being cool enough to appreciate the fact that these commercial pop guys were up to a Stratego-worthy standard of new wave. "Maneater" took the bassline from the Supremes' "You Can't Hurry Love"—it was pretty obvious, since Phil Collins had just covered the song and had a big hit with it.

But I love every minute of this song. The long, smoldering intro, building up tension beat by beat. The cheesy '80s sax solo to end all cheesy '80s sax solos. The way Oates utters that "oooh!" at the end of the sax solo. The way Hall utters the non-word "ooobaaddaaaswougghew!" at the precise four-minute mark. And the way it warns me about those tough girls they were always singing about. This girl was *deadly*, man, but she could really rip my world apart?

Why the hell didn't I meet any girls like this? Where did all these she-cats hang out? I was more than willing to be chewed up, digested and/or spat out by this heart-breaking, love-taking, dream-making maneater. Okay, so the beauty is there, but the beast is in her heart. Where's the downside, Hall? He wouldn't say. All he told me was "I wouldn't if I were you. I know what she can do." And all Oates added was "Watch out!" I have to admit, I was intrigued. But since she was a night creature, it was fairly unlikely she would wander over to Terry's house in the middle of our Stratego game. Oh well. I was a cautious Stratego player—always look for the bombs before you go looking for the flags. And as they say, lucky in Stratego, lame at love.

When I listen to "Maneater" now, it's on the Hall & Oates greatest hits album *Rock 'n Soul: Part 1*, which I stole from my sister Tracey. She won it off WHTT by calling in to the station as soon as she heard the intro to "Say It Isn't So," and the DJ announced her name on the air. (I got it on tape!) This added a level of unspeakable excitement to an already exciting record. Instead of stealing it when I went to college, I waited until Thanksgiving break, which allowed me to get away clean. I still don't know if she realizes where her copy is. But I do know she thought Hall was the cute one.

It's a little weird to listen to "Maneater" now and realize it reminds me of my sister. But songs that give out sensible advice, as most Hall & Oates songs do, always remind me of my sister Tracey, because she was the person in my life who made me smarter. Like Hall & Oates, she was fond of pointing out what a moron I was, and yet instead of making me defensive about it, she had a knack for convincing me how right she was. She is still exactly this way, and so is her eight-year-old daughter, Sarah, who already laughs at what a bad chess player I am. The last time I was able to fool my niece about anything was when I convinced her that the restaurant sign that says EMPLOYEES MUST WASH HANDS means it's illegal to wash your own, and even then she only bought it for about ten seconds.

When I was a little boy, I begrudged the way Tracey understood things I struggled to even see. When she would correct my grammar, I would call her Miriam Webster, who I thought in my childish ignorance was the author who wrote the dictionary. Tracey set me straight on that one too. Tracey is the sister who makes me less dumb. I spend a minute with her and she breathes in my dumb and breathes it back to me as smart. She does not even have to try to do this. Nobody else in my life has this same effect on me.

When I had my first apartment in Boston, I had Tracey over for tea. I was so proud of myself. I was a sophisticated man of the world, having my sister over to my place for tea. We sat on the couch, sipping from our Thermoses, enjoying a spread of EZ Cheez and Lorna Doones, as I said things like, "How are your classes going?"

As she was leaving, Tracey said, "Hey Rob, I don't know if you ever have, you know, girls over to the apartment?"

I didn't say anything.

"Buuuut, if you do? They really like the toilet paper to be on the little rolling thing."

"They do?"

"Yes. We do."

"The rolling thing that spins around?"

"Yes. They like the toilet paper hanging from the rolling thing."

"But you can reach it. It's just there on the sink and—"

"We just do."

"It's easier to—"

"We. Just. Do."

So I put the toilet paper on the rolling thing.

One of the things she keeps reminding me, often in so many words, is that my sisters are right. About everything.

But when you're a teenage boy, you can be narrow-minded about things that are girlie, things that are frivolous, things that are pop. Boys always want to be taken seriously, and they always want to transcend the tawdry emotion of the pop singer—it's a fairly standard response to the rigors of young manhood. You could trace it through the past century back to Ezra Pound in 1915 denouncing the lyric poem as unmanly in his hugely influential essay "The Serious Artist." The lyric was weak and feminine—a truly virile poet should be writing epics. This isn't so different from how people talk about culture now. Rock epics are for boys; pop hits are for girls. When you're a boy, pop is scary because it's a maneater. You sing along with a pop song, you turn into a girl. That takes some degree of emotional risk.

One of my new-wave idols, Scritti Politti's Green Gartside, used to tell a story about the days when he was an abrasive art-school punk. One night in the spring of 1980, he was at the Electric Ballroom in Manchester, England, talking to Joy Division's lead singer Ian Curtis, frustrated by the dead end of their doom-and-gloom musical styles. "I don't think I was able to offer him any solace, nor he I," Green said. "We were feeling pretty dejected and found our respective ways out of it."

A week later, Ian Curtis killed himself, and Green began playing disco. Ian Curtis's old bandmates went disco too, renaming themselves New Order. Green never looked back. As he proclaimed, "Fear of pop is an infantile disorder—you should face up to it like a man."

ROXY MUSIC

"More Than This"

1982

One thing we all learned from our radios in the '80s: Taking
Kenny Rogers's advice? Always a good idea.

Walk away from trouble when you can.

Don't fall in love with a dreamer.

Never count your money when you're sitting at the table.

Love the world away.

The best part of life is the thinnest slice.

Actually that last one was Air Supply, but it sure sounds like
something Kenny would say. I have no clue what it means, but like
everything Kenny says, it drips with the wisdom of a silver-fox
Zen sage.

Don't take your love to town.
It don't mean you're weak if you turn the other cheek.
Love will turn you around.

He sang this in the movie *Six Pack* to his foster family of zany orphans who tagged along on his stock-car racing adventures. This song turned Diane Lane from a child actress to the mature, grown bombshell she became in the film *Streets of Fire*, where she got to sing Meat Loaf songs to Willem Dafoe and the guy from *Eddie and the Cruisers*. Love *did* turn her around!

Sail away with me, to another world.

Most often, one does not sail to another world, especially if one is an island, and Dolly Parton is the other island in the stream. But do not argue back with Kenny. He doesn't need to hear your lip, buddy. K-Hova's been around the block, and he knows what ladies like to hear, and it isn't complaining about how they picked a fine time to leave you, with four hundred children and a crop in the field. Kenny knows how to give them what they want, without losing his mind. These are all good lessons, and I tried to learn them by heart. You got to know when to hold 'em, know when to fold 'em.

No woman made me break as many of these rules as Ms. Calasta.

Ms. Calasta always showed up late for class with a mug of coffee the size of a cinder block. She kept her hard pack of unfiltered cigarettes propped up on her desk, with a disturbing illustration of a salty old sea dog on the cover. My temples throbbed when she cleared her throat after a smoking break. I still dream of Ms. Calasta, who taught me so much, like the way modern literature reflected the alienation of a godless universe, and how if you hold your coffee mug at a certain angle, you can reduce a high school boy to Camembert.

She was a pheromone parfait in a pencil skirt, always rocking a severe bob of red hair and glasses that she could have used as a shiv. Years later, in my college French class, I would see the movie *Les Diaboliques* and realize that Ms. Calasta had stolen all her facial expressions from Simone Signoret. But it was all new to me. Where did she come from? How had she gotten this cool? Nobody knew, but we all worshipped her. The class was full of stoners, thespians, hockey players and bookworms, but everyone seemed to idolize Ms. Calasta. I was certain I loved her best.

It's always dangerous to have a crush on your teacher, because the crush filters into whatever you're supposed to be studying. Thanks to my Latin teacher, I will always feel a certain *nescio quid* whenever I will have used the future perfect tense (like just now). Whereas my crabby math teacher means that I will never truly enjoy full erotic release in the presence of a hypotenuse. Ms. Calasta had that effect on my reading and no doubt still does.

As near as I could guess, she hovered somewhere in her forties, looking back over her shadowy past with the elegant disdain of a 1930s bank robber in the back of the getaway car, glancing over the landscape as it trailed behind her. The clincher was her deep, hearty laugh, which involved downturned lips, a few seconds of sustained eye contact, a coda of hacks. Then she'd say the name of whoever made her laugh, as in, *Oh Raaahhhb*. Whatever she laughed at, you'd say again. She had a way of making you feel like an adult, as if you might slip up and she'd find out you were really just a sixteen-year-old boy reading *The Great Gatsby* for the first time. She would ask us questions like, "Have you ever argued about the death of God with someone you were sexually or romantically involved with?"

Not even Kenny Rogers could advise me how to handle this one. I could neither hold nor fold her.

Ms. Calasta laughed warmly at my enthusiasm for music and pop trash. She found it fetchingly jejune that I knew all the words to all the songs on the radio and read celebrity magazines. I even knew the oldies from the '50s and '60s that she'd grown up on.

"Oh, *Raaahhhb*," she said. "You have so much passion for the Shirelles. Tell me about that Skeeter Davis song again."

I was a dreamy boy, always bumping my head on ceiling fans and tripping over chairs, but she saw something in me that I hadn't seen in myself, and I became more like whoever she thought I was. She gladly read my stories, poems and plays. She listened to the tapes I made her. After hearing me gush about music, she called me "Dolores Haze," after the radio-listening, comics-reading nymphet in *Lolita*, but unfortunately, that was a joke I wouldn't get for years.

Like any teenager who reads *The Great Gatsby*, probably, I was madly in love with the teacher who had opened it up for me.

She was teaching us about Gatsby, the way he disappeared into his own Platonic conception of himself, the way he followed the green light at the end of Daisy's dock, drunk on the impossible past. But what did I know about the past? I didn't have one yet. I could only covet hers.

"Daisy and Gatsby had a connection," she mused. "But not sexually. Gatsby never could have fulfilled her." I wasn't sure what she meant, but I wrote it all down.

When I go up into my parents' attic and dig out my high school copies of these books, I am dumbstruck by all my feverish scrawls in the margin. I guess I really identified with the narrator of *Notes from Underground*. Looking at the novel now, the guy just seems every bit as much of a tool as I was, so either I was easier to impress then or I was just mesmerized by my frantic love for Ms. Calasta. I fished for details of her past, but instead I got more book recommendations, and devoured every one—John Milton's *Samson Agonistes*, Aldous Huxley's *After Many a Summer Dies the Swan*, Hemingway's *A Moveable Feast*.

This was also the period when I was cultivating arcane devotions to obscure saints. In a way, Catholic devotion was preparing me for my adulthood in the record collector/taper/critic world—collecting relics, obsessing over hagiography, looking for physical traces of the divine in the most ordinary things. It's no coincidence that so many record geeks grow up Catholic—it really prepares you for that path. Praying the rosary was twenty minutes, just like an album side. And it had five mysteries, just like (most often) the five songs on an album side.

When I discovered Roxy Music, it was like I'd been waiting to hear them all my life. Bryan Ferry took romantic obsession even beyond Kenny Rogers. Where Kenny had merely urged me to "Love the World Away," Bryan Ferry insisted that for the new-wave loveboy, the whole world would be obliterated by the sheer intensity of your devotion. Bryan Ferry wore a tuxedo and oozed ironic romantic despair. He had barely any voice at all, but his vocals were full of ornately stylized emotion; you could hear how many times he'd rehearsed every quiver, but somehow, that just made him more believable. "More than this," he whispered. "There's nothing."

This song was more than a hymn—it was a religion in itself. No wonder he did the video in a church, standing under a cross that only existed to shine light on him. And just like Gatsby, he took romantic obsession to the point where he disappeared into the Platonic conception of himself. He spends the video watching himself up there on a movie screen—an awkward, ungainly man dancing like a foxy disco lady. He clearly knew how funny he was, but all his emotional playacting didn't detract from his sincerity—it *was* his sincerity. He was a self-parodic Casanova in the privacy of his own mind, and every song was an invitation to the swinging party going on in his mirror—the more, the Bryan Ferrier.

I've loved this song since the first moment I heard it, yet I really have no idea who the girl is he's singing to or what she's like. I guess this is a song about desire so complete, it doesn't even need an actual girl in it. He is beyond such details. If she won't accept his love, he'll have to adore it himself. The end of the song is just

Bryan Ferry murmuring the words "more than this" and "nothing," so that every time, they describe a new shade of blue. Gatsby would have understood.

Thrillingly, Ms. Calasta answered the letters I wrote her from college, always beginning with "Dear, dear Rob." She got a little exasperated I was still calling her Ms. Calasta. Every time I was back home from college, I went over for coffee. One sunny afternoon, she taught me to smoke, on the barstools in her kitchen. She had the same hard pack with the same disturbing sea dog cartoon. I tried to seem nonchalant as my virgin lungs filled with smoke.

"This is pretty strong, Ms. Calasta."

"Yes, Rob."

"Where is your bathroom?"

"Upstairs. You could call me Catherine."

One day when I was in town, I called to invite myself over for coffee and cigarettes. But she was gone—she'd left abruptly, in a cloud of mystery. When asked about her whereabouts, other faculty members cleared their throats uncomfortably and changed the subject. Had she killed a man? Robbed a bank? Corrupted a student? (A student who wasn't me? Unthinkable!) Whoever knew wasn't talking, at least not to me. I would never find out. She left no trace, like the green light going dark at the end of Gatsby's dock, or like the siren on a Roxy Music record cover.

The Gatsby blues made so much sense to me in Ms. Calasta's class. When I read the book as an adult, I was startled to see that Gatsby and Daisy have only known each other for five years. When I was sixteen, this seemed like a lifetime's worth of tragic romance. I'd always cherished Gatsby and Daisy as the emblem of a doomed, fatal, endless romantic obsession. They'd met, they'd fallen in love, they'd endured a tragic separation, but he had carried the torch for her all this time. But it was just five freaking years? I'm an adult now—I can do five years standing on my head.

But as Gatsby knew, five years *is* a long time. That's the time the boy and girl have spent together in the Human League's "Don't You Want Me," easily the most famous breakup song in history. They've had five years together, and now she's got the world at her feet and she's leaving him behind. That's how long we've got until the planet burns out in Bowie's "Five Years." It's how long John Wayne wanders the wilderness looking for Natalie Wood in *The Searchers*. It's how long Ione Skye and her dad have lived together in *Say Anything*.

Odysseus and Circe got five years in *The Odyssey*, so do Humbert and Dolores in *Lolita*, so do Axl Rose and his Sunset Strip groupie in "You Could Be Mine." There's something primal about that time span. Five years doesn't seem quite as epic as it did back then, when it was a third of my life. But I still get it. LCD Soundsystem sang about it in "All My Friends": "You spent five long years trying to get with the plan, and the next five years trying to be with your friends again." By the time you're an adult, you're used to seeing friends disappear into their five-year plans. They drop out to get married, have babies, go to grad school, get divorced. They start a band or enter the penal system. They vanish for years at a time—some come back, some don't. Some of them you wait for and some you let go.

Sometimes the only way they come back is in a song. Sometimes the song is the green light at the end of the dock, a sign that the dream we've been chasing is already behind us, in the past. Sometimes when a girl goes away, the conversation doesn't end. You keep talking to her, just in case she can hear.

So we beat on, boats against the current, borne ceaselessly back into Bryan Ferry.

"Total Eclipse of the Heart"

People rarely threaten to kill me these days. That's one of the weird things about being an adult. It's illegal, so it just doesn't happen very often. In the past few years, only two other guys have threatened me with murder, and neither time was all that alarming. One guy got mad at me in the accountant's office when I was getting my taxes done. I was on crutches at the time, because of the tragic roller-disco crash of '05 (don't aaaask), and he tripped over my legs on his way to use the waiting-room coffee machine, which hasn't worked since the Clinton administration. Enraged by the denial of coffee, he threw the Styrofoam cup at me and said, "I'm gonna fucking kill you." It was a weird threat to make, depending on how you rate Styrofoam murder weapons. It could be done, killing a man with Styrofoam, but it would require some degree of premeditation—carving a styro-scimitar, or maybe a blowgun to shoot those little peanuts. But for your garden-variety impulse killing, Styrofoam gets you nowhere, especially in Brooklyn. His wife made him come back over and apologize, which was embarrassing for both of us.

The other guy was on an Amtrak train, using his cell phone in the quiet car. I usually avoid the quiet car because I loathe hearing myself chew, but this time I was in it, and although I didn't mind this clod's moronic conversation (reading the *Star* out loud), I couldn't stand the slow exhales and exasperated sighs of my spineless fellow passengers. I always regard a succinct and informative shoosh as morally superior to an hour of feeble throat-clearing, and as a longtime librarian, I pride myself on my nonconfrontational shooshing skills. But my professional expertise must have failed me, because this guy took it hard, particularly after other passengers joined in. He waited till we were on the escalator at Penn Station to utter those same five magic words, "I'm gonna fucking kill you." It was hard to take him seriously, since it would have been *much* easier to kill me on the train. I mean, getting thrown from a moving train would be kind of hot. A very Robert Mitchum way to go. But escalator killings? No class.

Strange as it may sound, though, whenever I hear those words, it always makes me feel all warm and gushy inside. It whisks me back in time to the golden summer of 1983, when I worked on a garbage truck with a bunch of other guys. We threatened to kill one another all the time. In fact, we considered the day a waste if nobody did any heavy bleeding.

There was me, Soup, Okie, Psycho and Psycho's brother, Chicken. They called me "Bones." Our truck driver, a crusty old Irish guy named Harry, called us all the same name, which was "You faggots." We were picking up garbage on the Southeast Expressway, working for the Massachusetts Highway Department, out of the Granite Avenue barracks. We had our orange vests, our plastic bags and our idiot sticks—you know, the stick with the little pointy spike at the tip for spearing trash. Every morning, we'd pile in the back of the truck and Harry would drive us to some point in the road, drop us off, then go get a beer.

We cleaned the sides of the expressway between Exit 11 and Exit 20, the southern stretch, all the way from the Central Artery in downtown Boston to Furnace Brook Parkway in Quincy. We covered every grimy inch of I-93, the six-lane monster connecting Boston to the South Shore, down the Neponset River, through Savin Hill, beneath the Boston Gas tanks with the rainbow paintings. We cleaned the living fuck out of that place. We speared all the garbage that piles up along the side of any highway: porno mags, plastic bags, Burger King wrappers, crushed drink cups, beer cans, the occasional pair of pants.

At the end of the day, with our truck loaded with garbage bags, Harry would drive us all to the dump, and we'd usually "go to the Qs for a jump," which meant swimming in the quarries. Everybody had a story about dead bodies in the water, and Psycho claimed there were dead horses in it, but everyone swam in the stew anyway. That's usually when damage would get done with those idiot sticks. Blood might get shed, but never tears.

It was hard work but it meant being outside in the summer sun, which made it a perfect job. We took an aggressive attitude toward garbage, which meant that frequently the crew would tie rags around their heads like the soldiers in *Apocalypse Now* and head under the expressway exit ramps doing the war chant, which was the opening lines of Def Leppard's "Rock of Ages" (Rise up! Gather round! Rock this place to the ground!), which in retrospect was somewhat doofy. We would stand around, talk shit about one another and use our idiot sticks to write the words "Fuck Harry" in the dirt. Soup would always draw the Blue Öyster Cult logo. Then Psycho would say, "Hey, Soup, how's your mom, the Black and Decker Pecker Wrecker," and more blood would get shed.

I could not believe how cool it felt to wear the orange vest of pride. It was the garb of a working man. I had never felt before like I was part of a gang of guys. It was like being in the cast of *The Great Escape*—I got excited driving to work every day. These guys were from all over town: Psycho and Chicken were from Dorchester, Soup from Southie, Okie from Quincy and me from Milton. Okie was the one with the radio. I brought my Walkman the first day of work, but I never put it on, partly because I knew Harry would think it was goofing off, partly because I knew Soup and Okie would liberate me from it, but mainly because it was more fun to listen to a bunch of other seventeen-year-old males shoot the shit. We once spent an entire day debating whether you could kill a guy by biting off his thumb. Soup said the guy would bleed to death. Okie said the guy's blood would clot, so he wouldn't die in time, and he could use his other thumb to gouge out your eyes. Psycho just giggled.

Psycho was probably the guy who knew from experience, but he never said much—he just laughed all the time, with flashing eyes that made everyone a little more scared of him than the others. We all just said, "That guy Psycho is fried." When we were in the back of the truck, Psycho liked to beat on the roof and yell, "Onward!" Harry wouldn't have taken that from the rest of us, but even he was too creeped out by Psycho to say anything.

The day revolved around the coffee breaks at the Dunkin' Donuts on Morrissey Boulevard. The radio was always playing "The Safety Dance," with that *boop-boop-beep* one-finger synth loop blasting behind the counter. If Harry was at the counter with us, we'd listen to him tell us he was sick and tired of our goofing off. If Harry brought his friend Red, the supervisor of another truck crew, we'd listen to Red's Vietnam stories. Sometimes Harry brought Frankie, who only knew how to say one sentence: "The only thing I give a fuck about is bucks, booze and broads—in that order!" For lunch, Harry dropped us at the McDonald's on Gallivan Boulevard while he went to the Eire Pub across the street. I would listen in on the Soup-Okie debates.

"You're such a bitch-off, I can't believe I'm even talking to you."

"Bitch-off? There's no such thing as a bitch-off."

"Yes there is, and you are one."

"No, I'm saying there's no such word. Nobody says bitch-off."

"I'm saying it."

"No, I mean, it isn't even a fake word. Nobody says it as a name to call somebody. You just made it up."

"Fuck you, bitch-off. Don't you know that song? Billy Joel. You had to be a bitch-off, didn't cha? Oh no, you had to be a bitch-off. Don't come bitching to me, you big bitch-off."

"I've changed my mind. You are such a fucking bitch-off."

One day in July, Harry told us things were going to be different. We had a new crew member. She was Kelly Ryan, and Harry told us her dad knew somebody. So there were rules: nobody was supposed to talk to Kelly Ryan, look at Kelly Ryan or bother Kelly Ryan. There was a girl on our truck now. Kelly Ryan showed up her first day wearing makeup and a cute little miniskirt, with Bonnie Tyler blond hair. Lots of girls had the Bonnie Tyler hair that summer.

Kelly Ryan basically ruined everything, because all anyone tried to do now was put each other down to impress Kelly Ryan, which would have required an Act of God and not merely a bunch of hormonally crazed seventeen-year-old boys in orange vests. That first day, when we piled off the truck to clean the Casimir Pulaski Memorial Underpass, Kelly stayed behind, sitting on the truckbed, dangling her legs and reading *Harper's Bazaar*. Nobody complained to Harry about Kelly Ryan not working. The crew got a lot more violent.

Kelly Ryan seemed like what they used to call "stuck up." She never talked to her coworkers on the back of the truck. At Dunkin' Donuts, she sat at the other end of the counter and pretended not to know us, even though she had the same matching orange vest. She never had a nice word. Every time she opened her mouth, it was like she gave birth to a litter of bitch-kitties.

After work on Wednesday, Kelly Ryan talked to me for the first time, because I had a car. She needed a ride home from work. She lived in Quincy, but I was happy to make the trip, especially since I knew it would piss off Okie, because he also had a car but she did not ask him for a lift. I didn't know why she picked me, but I assumed it had something to do with being "sweet." Teenage boys do not necessarily like it when girls tell them they're "sweet," because it means they're safe, but I did not have a problem with this.

I had never driven a girl around in my car before. It was the brown '74 Chevy Nova with no windshield wipers and the floor rusted clean through. I had driven around with guy friends, which was no problem, because teenage boys are vaguely excited by the risk of losing a limb if you get your shoe caught in the hole. But I could tell it had been a while since Kelly had been in a car this crummy.

"Nice car," she said. "You got brakes in this thing?"

"Used to. Now I just drag my feet, like the Flintstones."

"Do the windows go down?"

"Mine does."

"Great. My boyfriend's car has this thing called air-conditioning."

"Never heard of it. How's your boyfriend?"

"Fine. Tomorrow's our three-month anniversary."

"Well, not *reeeally*. '*Annus*' means 'year.'"

"Excuse me?"

"It's Latin. Technically you can't have a three-month anniversary, because '*annus*' means 'year.' As in 'annual,' or '*annuit coeptis*.'"

"Right. What about anus?"

"That's different. They're not etymologically related."

"But you're related to an anus. As in, you are totally an anus."

"You have a point. This is your street?"

"Let me off at the curb."

"Technically, I guess it's your quarter-anniversary."

"The curb."

The next day, everyone on the truck knew I'd given Kelly Ryan a ride home, and there was a vague sense of aggro in the air. Nobody could figure out why she picked me. Kelly Ryan, as usual, didn't say hi to anyone, and sat in the back of the truck, reading her fashion mags. We cleaned up alongside the breakdown lanes on Savin Hill and debated which of the models on her fashion mags was hotter, Christie Sprinkley or Paulina Pork Her All Over.

Now that Kelly had seen the inside of my car, I assumed she wouldn't bum any more rides—and now that she'd seen the inside of my personality, I assumed she would never speak to me again. But I still had a car, and she still needed a lift.

"Where's your boyfriend?"

"His car is in the shop. His car, which has air-conditioning."

"Are you going out tonight?"

"Yeah, I don't know. I didn't call him. I've been procrastinating all day."

A few exits went by before I spoke up again. "'*Cras*' means 'tomorrow,' by the way."

"What are you talking about?"

"'*Pro cras*' is Latin. It means 'for tomorrow.' So technically you can't procrastinate till tonight."

"Thanks for clearing that up. What's Latin for douchebag?"

"*Ecce homo.*"

"Ever heard of the word 'vagina'?"

"That's Latin too. Caesar uses that word in the *Gallic Wars*. I mean, I know what that word means. I know all about it, you know? I'm just making conversation here."

"Please don't."

"What do you want to talk about then?"

"Just don't say anything and I won't either. And fifteen or twenty minutes will go by, extremely fucking painful minutes, but then we'll be in Boston and I will get out of this car and take an aspirin or something."

So I didn't say anything.

The next day, she told Harry she hated the garbage truck, and if he didn't find an office job for her at the barracks, her dad was going to break his legs. Friday was our last day of Kelly Ryan, and we had a vague sense of detumescence. We knew we were still going to insult one another's mothers and threaten to stab one another, but it wasn't going to be as much fun. After lunch, Chicken went for Okie with his idiot stick and drew blood, and even that couldn't cheer us up.

Friday was the last day Kelly Ryan needed a ride home, and also the first day she didn't even ask, just showed up at my car. I did a pretty good job of not talking. I turned on the radio and she looked out the window. We were cruising north on the expressway, the same stretch of road we'd been cleaning up all week. Then I cleared my throat.

"Am I always going to be this way?"

"What?"

I repeated my question. "Am I always going to be this way?"

I was as surprised as she was. I was surprised I'd said it, but I was even more surprised she took a second to think about it.

"Yes," she said eventually. "You are always going to be this way. It's okay, though. Some girls are probably this way too."

"Great. Do you know any?"

"Shhh. It's the tunnel."

We rolled into the Callahan Tunnel. She held her breath. In ordinary traffic, from one end of the tunnel to the other is a minute and twenty seconds. Some girls can hold their breath all the way through the tunnel. Kelly Ryan had her lips clenched and her eyes closed. There was no radio in the tunnel, so the only sound I could hear was Kelly holding her breath. I knew she was going to make it to the other side.

HAYSI FANTAYZEE

"Shiny Shiny"

1983

Now, really. Haysi Fantayzee. When the good Lord was handing out brain soup, these guys must have shown up with a fork. Any discussion of this group has to start with a few basic questions: (1) who were they? (2) what kind of idiot actually listened to this shit? and (3) how in the blood-spattered name of the lords and the creatures could such a musical atrocity happen?

The first one is easy—they were an English new-wave duo who had one hit in 1983 called "Shiny Shiny." The third one is easy too—we do not live in an ideal universe, and our tribe is a sewer of vanity and corruption, and songs like "Shiny Shiny" are the wounds we bear from our cosmic floggings. The second one is kind of hard, though. The only answer I can come up with is "me," but since there were clearly a lot of other people out there who paid actual money for Haysi Fantayzee records, that's just not an adequate answer.

I don't meet a lot of other Haysi Fantayzee fans. Sometimes I've played the song for people who respond, "Hmmm, this is interesting," but in a way that's more like "There are two exits in this room, the window and the door. If this song doesn't end soon, I'm going to opt for the window." So the possibility remains that for all intents and purposes, *nobody* likes this song. That's fine with me. It's part of being a fan—sometimes it's a lonely thing to devote your heart to a song, especially when it's a song that literally nobody can stand, from an idiotic group with an idiotic name and idiotic haircuts. Everybody's got something like this in their life, whether it's a song nobody else likes or a celebrity crush everybody else finds hideous or a team that always loses. We all have our Haysi Fantayzees. Do we choose them or do they choose us?

One-hit wonders are a noble breed. It's a fallacy that artists should have long, productive careers. William Wordsworth invented modern poetry in one ten-year bang, 1795 to 1805, but then he was cashed out, although he lived to write utter rubbish for another forty-five years. Walt Whitman wrote American literature's most towering achievements between 1855 and 1865, and then sucked for the next twenty-seven years. T. S. Eliot? Spent the twentieth century dining out on a handful of poems from his 1915–1925 hot streak. Rock stars did not invent burning out. They just do it louder.

It's hard to guess in advance which one-hit wonders are going to go on to be famous for their hit and which are going to be obscure. If you asked around in 1983, or for that matter, 1993, nobody would have guessed that Kajagoogoo would one day be remembered as a consummate '80s one-hit wonder. Their song has gone on to everlasting life. (I actually thought their second single, "Hang On Now," was in some ways a more thought-provoking and inspiring statement of the Kajagoogoo ethos.) Anyway, everybody who likes pop music knows the hits by Kajagoogoo and Dexy's Midnight Runners and Tommy Tutone. But not Haysi Fantayzee or Total Coelo or the Belle Stars. I'm not here to argue that they *should* be more famous than they are; I'm just asking why.

This applies to one-hit wonders of all eras, of course. For instance, every year I hear "Brandy (You're a Fine Girl)" and "Play That Funky Music" more times than I heard them in the entire 1970s combined. These songs are much more famous and popular now than they were when they were actual hits. "Y.M.C.A." was a hit for about a month, then vanished for more than a decade, but you will probably hear it at some point in the next week, especially if you attend a wedding, a baseball game, or a mud-wrestling match. Whereas the biggest one-hit job of the 1970s, and in fact the decade's biggest hit, was Debbie Boone's "You Light Up My Life," which I haven't heard since it came out. How come "Y.M.C.A." lives forever, while "Undercover Angel" and "Heaven on the 7th Floor" disappear completely from our collective memory? Some songs get pimped on soundtracks, commercials and sporting events, while other equally popular songs sail away like Brandy's sailor boyfriend. Nobody knows how this works. The gods of pop music are fickle bastards.

But it's different when we talk about the '80s, because the era's one-hit wonders are by far the era's most loved songs, and in fact, if you mention "'80s music" to someone, they probably assume you're talking about Kajagoogoo or Dexy's Midnight Runners or Men Without Hats. Styx were infinitely more popular than these groups at the time, and had a lot more hits. Yet the music we remember as typifying the era is the stuff that seemed most frivolous and temporary at the time.

Which brings us to Haysi Fantayzee. Man oh man, did I love this band. "Shiny Shiny" was their anthem: a boy and a girl, two Brit kids who looked like they just got lobotomized with knitting needles, wearing midriff shirts and top hats and dreadlocks, chanting about nuclear war over a bouncy little jump-rope riff, rapping lines like "I'm a hot retard / Marquis de Sade!" There's a fiddle solo. Every time you think the song's about to end, they rip into another chorus, yelping "Shiny shiny, bad times behind me / Shiny shiny, sha na na na." The boy was named Jeremy Healy; the girl was Kate Garner. "Shiny Shiny" hit number sixteen in the U.K. and never charted here, but it got a fair amount of MTV airplay. The album was called *Battle Hymns for Children Singing*, and included a sixteen-page comic book of the two Haysi kids looking alienated over street scenes, and looking naked while looking alienated. They sang in a made-up language of brain-damaged slang like "John Wayne Is Big Leggy," which is a critique of U.S. imperialism as well as a song about kinky sex, and their major existential statement, "I Lost My Dodi."

They were one of the bands that sent me frothing to the

fan mags, devouring any scrap of information I could get. I was thrilled to read that Jeremy kept a wheelchair in his apartment, which he'd nicked from a local hospital. There wasn't anything wrong with him; he was just lazy. That had to be every teen boy's biggest fantasy, at least in the non–Phoebe Cates division.

I was intrigued by their ideas on politics and the impending end of the world. I thrilled when they picked fights with other pop stars, like a synth duo I'd never heard of called Mirror Mirror; according to Kate Garner, "It made a mockery of the idea of a video band. Their image was lousy." I had no idea it was even *possible* to make a mockery out of what the Haysis represented, but I guess it was—they took not being taken seriously very seriously.

From the fan mags, I knew Jeremy used to live with Boy George in London, where they would have loud public fights over hair spray. Kate was a fashion photographer having a bash at pop stardom. They were scenesters from the artsy milieu that gathered around the Blitz nightclub; they explained that "Shiny Shiny" was about nuclear apocalypse, and that their clothes were inspired by literary influences such as Charles Dickens, with his portrayal of Victorian street scruffs in novels like *Oliver Twist*. (Boy George, in his biography, said Jeremey was "Dickensian . . . with the emphasis on 'dick,'" which could only be a compliment.)

There was a third member of the group who didn't sing, but who apparently did nothing besides think about the Haysi Fantayzee attitude of life and make statements to the press giving updates on their opinions, like "The one thing we all had in common was a dislike of doom-laden electronics," or "I'm very sick of doom. There was a whole couple of years of it, that feeling of romanticism in wandering amongst the atomic ruins and being noble when the world is collapsing around you." But I never noticed he existed. His picture was on the *back* cover of the album, so who cares? New-wave attention spans are short.

There were loads of philosopher kings who got a lot more respect and attention than these clowns—the Police, for example, who I also loved. The difference is that the Police were a rock band, while Haysi Fantayzee was a pop group, so Sting's ideas about Jung and Nabokov and the Loch Ness Monster were taken more seriously than whatever drivel Haysi Fantayzee were rapping about.

It would suit my argument perfectly if Haysi Fantayzee made better records than the Police did, but I like music better than arguments, so I'm going to have to concede that point. The Police had lots of good songs; the Haysis didn't. But the Police never peaked as high as "Shiny Shiny." I play it more than I play all the Police songs combined.

I expected a lot more from Haysi than this one song. I thought they were the future of something. I was moved when *People* magazine reviewed *Battle Hymns for Children Singing* in their Picks & Pans section, and said, "They do, though, seem to represent an unrest that demands to be recognized." But I can't claim it got that recognition, really. The group fizzled out not long after "Shiny Shiny." They never made a sequel and left their fans hanging, children singing waiting for more battle hymns. They went on to fame and fortune in their different fields. Kate Garner kept rising as a photographer—she took the cover photo for Sinéad O'Connor's *The Lion and the Cobra*—and Jeremy Healy became a huge U.K. techno DJ, scoring a hit with his 1990 Clash remix "Return to Brixton," and joining E-Z Posse for the lowest-common-denominator acid-house cash-in novelty hit imaginable, "Everything Starts with an E." He ended up marrying the English starlet Patsy Kensit, becoming her fourth rock-star husband, after Oasis's Liam Gallagher, Simple Minds' Jim Kerr and a guy from Big Audio Dynamite.

Both are still successful and acclaimed and doing nothing at all that would remind anyone of this group they used to be in. It's safe to say all regard "Shiny Shiny" as a youthful indiscretion, a blot on otherwise laudable careers full of artistic achievement, and wish people would forget this song ever happened. Why stir up the ashes? Why make trouble? Why not let sleeping one-hit wonders lie?

Because the song is too damn good, that's why. It's a Taj Majal of awesome, a basilica of No Fucking Way.

Most groups, after recording a hit this transcendently ridiculous, would run for the hills and try to atone, like Kajagoogoo or Haircut One Hundred after they ditched their pop-idol lead singers, remade themselves into tastefully mature jazz-rock combos, and slipped into quality nothingness. It was a big letdown to find out that Kajagoogoo were big Steely Dan and Joni Mitchell fans who wanted nothing more than to climb out of the teen-pop ghetto as fast as they could. Nick Beggs even told *Smash Hits* their name was based on infant language. "Goo-ga-ga-goo was the first thing that came into my mind. I didn't like the goo-ga-ga part and went for something more casual. So Kajagoogoo. The sound of primal life, don't you know." Yeah, *real* primal. But once they ditched the "goo goo" and started calling themselves Kaj, they lost their dodi.

Haysi Fantayzee had no "We hope you like our new direction" phase. They blew it out, in true "Shiny shiny, bad times behind me" style. They went down in a blaze of glory. But that suits the song. That's part of their beauty. They were phonies who never sold out their phoniness.

I wonder why phonies spoke to my teen self more profoundly than . . . truies? But they did. I suppose it goes back to the time I spent in the hospital when I was eight. Six weeks is a long time to be laid up with pneumonia when you're that age, and I was often too feverish to read, and the TV in my hospital room only had a couple of channels. But I got *The Banana Splits* every day at four. I bonded with the Splits. Fleegle had the power to heal. In case you don't remember, the Banana Splits were four animals playing in a . . . okay, guys in animal costumes, pretending to be a rock band, living in a wacky psychedelic clubhouse. It's one of those drugged-out '70s kiddie shows that has an unexpected afterlife in reruns, much like *Scooby Doo*. Fleegle (the dog), Bingo (the ape), Drooper (the lion) and Snorky (the elephant) were a jungle culture club, and I found them immensely comforting.

Their best song was "You Can't Buy Soul"—for some reason, the Banana Splits really liked to sing about soul, a surprising fixation for a band comprised of cartoon characters. But they had other great songs too, like "I Enjoy Being a Boy" and "Doin' the Banana Split," both of which were on a special 45 single you could cut out from the back of a Frosted Flakes box. A lot of talent and energy went into these tunes, much more than anybody should have felt obliged to give, considering they were never going to get the credit and that nobody past puberty would hear it. I felt bad for Snorky, who never got to talk (much less sing), but merely played keyboards. I had so much time on my hands in the hospital, so I wrote customized verses for him to sing in their songs. (I never got around to mailing them in to the band because . . . well, at a certain point, I realized he was just an elephant. They don't talk.)

There was something soothing about the Banana Splits, even knowing they weren't real animals—I was too young then to know who Oscar Wilde was, or what he meant when he said, "Give me a mask and I'll speak the truth," but I knew what Fleagle and crew were trying to say. "I Enjoy Being a Boy" was such a beautiful song, it was as if they had to disappear behind the animals in order to sing it or they'd shrivel up. It was as if the Splits were the only boys who felt safe speaking the truth about what they enjoyed about being a girl, which was being with a girl. The Splits were hugely different—realer—than the boys I knew at school, with their endless dumbness and meanness. It was good training for a pop fan, since I didn't worry too much about what was going into the music; I was just enjoying what came out.

All kiddie shows had rock bands in those days: Josie and the Pussycats, the Archies, the Chan Clan, Lancelot Link and the Evolution Revolution, Fat Albert and the Junkyard Band. They'd sing a song at the end of the episode to remind us all what we'd learned. Sometimes it got pretty freaky, as in the glam-rock weirdness of Kaptain Kool and the Kongs. There was one episode of *Electra Woman and Dyna Girl* where they had to save the world from an evil madman genius named Glitter Rock, who wore a rainbow-colored Afro wig and threatened to cause massive destruction with each strum of his guitar.

All these fake bands gave me a preference for pop stars who rejected the pose of naturalism, the pose of really-meaning-it. There's probably a direct correlation between all the cartoon bands I grew up loving as a little kid in the '70s and the new-wave poseurs I loved in the '80s. The Banana Splits didn't look any more ridiculous pretending to play guitars than Missing Persons did.

There were tons of nuclear-annihilation songs back then, but for some reason, the one that I still shudder for is the one by the biggest phonies around. Haysi Fantayzee left absolutely nothing behind that anybody could conceivably build on, least of all themselves. That's how pop trash works. So as to the question we started with—"What kind of idiot actually listened to this shit?"—it still seems to remain a mystery. It's one of the mysteries that makes "Shiny Shiny" the quintessential artifact of a unique moment in the history of this pitiful planet.

"John Wayne Is Big Leggy," though? That one blows.

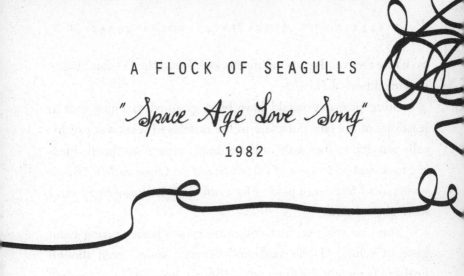

A FLOCK OF SEAGULLS
"Space Age Love Song"
1982

There are times in a man's life that can only be described as "times in a man's life." The first time he experiences A Flock of Seagulls is one of them.

It was my first rock concert: A Flock of Seagulls, the Fixx and the Police at Sullivan Stadium in Foxboro, Massachusetts, in August of 1983. The master of ceremonies was everybody's favorite MTV personality, Martha Quinn. I tagged along with my sister Tracey and her friends, one of whom drove us in his Pontiac Parisienne station wagon. Since this was the *Synchronicity* tour sponsored by MTV, there was a giant video screen playing MTV all day between the bands. It was a long, hot afternoon in the bleachers, but fortunately I'd brought a book in my back pocket.

So while the couples around me necked, I read the Pelican Shakespeare edition of *Hamlet*.

Sting probably would have been gratified to know that at least one of his fans out there in the nosebleed seats was psychically wandering the castle in Elsinore in preparation for the literary rock-and-roll rigors of "Don't Stand So Close to Me." But it wasn't like I felt out of place—far from it. *Au contraire mon frere*, I felt right at home.

The Fixx went on first, committing the classic touring-band gaffe of yelling "Hello Foxboro!" between songs, even though Foxboro is merely the town where Boston keeps its local football stadium. Since I was curious about the right and wrong ways to comport myself at a musical event, I studied the crowd—some people were standing up, but most people were sitting down. The guy right in front of me kept yelling for "Saved by Zero," as if he were worried they weren't going to play it, after huddling backstage: "I don't know, lads—maybe we should skip the hit this afternoon?"

The Police headlined, by which point it was dark and everybody was standing up. Martha Quinn came on to introduce the band and ask, "Is everybody ready to see the Police? I can't hear you! Is everybody ready! To see! The Police!" It was an intensely moving experience, with everybody dancing while Sting sang "hee-yo, hee-yo-yo" for two hours. I had never seen the everybody-raises-their-lighters scene before, and it took my breath away. It was the same communal thrill I'd experienced in the dark of the Madrid *discotecas*, except it was outdoors under a starry sky.

But it was the Flock who moved me most that fine day. The singer wore a fetching powder-blue jumpsuit, darting from side to side behind his keyboard. Even from half a mile away, it was easy to see their bleached bat-wing haircuts wiggle as they performed their huge hit ("I Ran"), their medium-size hits ("Space Age Love Song," "Wishing"), and assorted non-hits that nobody except me sang along to ("Telecommunications," "It's Not Me Talking"). The 'Gulls never had a chance, getting stuck in the middle spot, their hair wilting in the dog-day afternoon sun before a jaded crowd that was already exhausted waiting to see the headliners. But they gave it all they had.

Not everybody was into the music part of the event. In fact, the couple two rows ahead of me completely ignored A Flock of Seagulls and spent the whole set going to second. (Or at least what second base was in 1983. I couldn't even guess what second base means now. A foursome that doesn't involve dairy products?) But it was a glorious night. Back in the Parisienne, as we waited in line in the parking lot traffic jam, *Synchronicity* played in the tape deck so we could sing along with all the Stingian odes to Jungian mythology we'd just heard. It took us three "Miss Gradenko"s to even get out of the parking lot. *Hamlet* was excellent too.

But the thing I carried around with me most from that day was the sensation of dissolving into a crowd of other people. I didn't even make an excuse to go back and hide in the car. At any kind of party or social gathering, I was a pro at borrowing the keys from my ride, on the pretext of having left something in the back-seat, and then staying there with my book until it was time to go home. I felt an immense debt of gratitude to my sister, Sting, the Dark Prince of Denmark and Martha Quinn. But especially to the Flock, who had gotten less love than anyone that day, despite working harder for it.

What I didn't comprehend, and wouldn't for years, is that America was the only country in the world where anybody liked the Fixx or A Flock of Seagulls. Despite the fact that they seemed like certifiable English new-wave groups, they had *no* fans back home. Not until I went to college, and met people who actually came from England, did I grasp the gap between what English people like and what Anglophile American teen twits like. "I Ran" didn't even make the Top 40 in the U.K., and the only time they came close to a real hit there was "Wishing (If I Had a Photograph of You)." But in the United States, they had that exotic appeal of being an English band, and we imagined hordes of foxy British mod girls chasing the Flock down the street. It was painful to realize that this had never happened to A Flock of Seagulls, and therefore was that much more unlikely to happen to any Flock of Seagulls fan.

Everybody remembers the hair. They were the first famous rock group ever to have started out as hairdressers—and they definitely saved their best work for themselves. Even a big fan of their music, like me, has to concede the point that these days, they are remembered mostly because of the coiffures. That's only fair, because the hair helped get them noticed, and it's the main reason they sum up the Bad Hair Era for so many people. If you're making fun of somebody for having new-wave hair, the words "You!

Flock of Seagulls!" are going to come up. John Doe of X accused them of making money with "a haircut and a disco beat." The hair made them a legend, but it trapped them in an image they could never escape. It became a peroxide prison camp.

My friends' band opened for A Flock of Seagulls once in the '90s, in Richmond, Virginia. But I didn't go because I suspected it would be depressing, and apparently I was right—whoever was in the Flock at that moment was reportedly dour and hostile to my friends. The Flock had heard so many nasty jokes, they had the wariness you often see in ex-celebrities, where they always suspect there's somebody in the corner talking shit. That's a sad thing in itself. Like Scott Baio's reality show where he revealed that whenever he's in public, he assumes people are making fun of him, and he goes ballistic if he thinks he hears the word "Chachi." How sad is that? But you can see how it happens.

When you see the Flock of Seagulls guys on TV now in any kind of '80s retrospective show, they're wearing baseball caps, as if to say, "This is what you have done to us. You took all the fun out of hair for us. We have shaved our domes as penance. Happy?"

If you watch their videos now, you can see it in their eyes. They sang "Space Age Love Song" because they suspected outer space was the only place they would ever find the right girl. I hope they found her somewhere.

In the video for "I Ran," they stand on a tiny soundstage that seems to be draped in Hefty bags. They have a couple of mirrors and some smoke, as well as two ladies wearing their own Hefty-bag ensembles. When I was seventeen, I thought this video was a conceptually bold statement about technology and alienation. But now it looks like a public-access production of *The Cabinet of Dr. Caligari*. But I still love it. And I still love them—for helping me blend into that crowd and feel, for the first time, like I was meant to be there. You can kill the dream—but you cannot kill the hair.

CHAKA KHAN

"I Feel for You"

1984

Karaoke and the '80s are basically the same thing. Nobody knows why exactly, but it's true.

You know what else is true? We're in a basement karaoke bar on Avenue A with a hot microphone, cold vodka and the lights out. I am Chaka Khan. I am Taylor Dayne. I am Sheena Easton. My sugar walls stand higher than yours.

"He said, Honey, what's wrooong with you?"

Ally presses the buzzer on the wall to summon the waiter back with more drinks.

"Nations go to war over women like you."

I always end up doing the Sheena Easton songs, the really

slutty ones. If I don't punch them into the machine myself, Ally will punch them in for me. I can't help it.

"Strut! Pout! Put it out!"

The waiter takes too long with the drinks. But we're not going anywhere.

"Come spend the night inside my sugar walls!"

We always seem to crash at Sing Sing in the East Village with our fellow karaoke-whore friends. Everybody does songs from the '80s. Ally does LL Cool J's "Going Back to Cali," rapping about hitting on chicks on the West Coast. She does Prince's "Darling Nikki," a song about picking up a freaky girl who likes to grind.

Ally always does songs by men, and I always do songs by women. It's not a rule, just the pattern we fall into. She especially loves to sing the Boy George songs, because she has the same low, throaty voice. I love to see her flicker her switchblade eyelashes when she sings "Do You Really Want to Hurt Me."

Our friends are our karaoke whores—we know how to find one another. It usually starts with dinner, then over coffee Ally whispers something to Caryn, and Caryn whispers something to Jennie, and Nils and I wonder what the ladies are plotting. It always involves Sing Sing and a private room. You can stand at the bar and sing, but that means waiting your turn. When you get a private room, you and your crew just punch your own songs into the machine. No waiting, just singing. There's no clock in the room, and no window, so you have no sense of time passing.

If you're shy, you can sing sitting down, but none of us are shy when we're here, in our rented room in the dark. I never sit down—I come here to strut, pout, put it out.

All our karaoke fiends have their jams. Melissa does the Madonna songbook. Niki goes for Stevie Nicks epics like "Sara." Nils owns the Lionel Richie tunes, because their voices are in the same range. Nobody else tries Lionel Richie when Nils is around; I used to sing "Easy," but I had to knock it off. Caryn and I always want to sing the same Ashlee Simpson song, "La La," so it's a race to see who grabs the mike first. Kevin does Chaka Khan so well, he stole "I Feel for You" from me. But one of these nights, I'm stealing it back.

Part of the fun of karaoke is the hangover the next day, flipping through my notebook to see which titles and songbook numbers I jotted down. Oh yeah, "Total Eclipse of the Heart"! That was our jam. Wait, who did "My Prerogative" last night?

But it's always songs from the 1980s. Spend any time in a karaoke bar, and you will hear the same two songs over and over: "Don't Stop Believin'" and "Livin' on a Prayer." A boy-girl couple might interrupt with "Don't You Want Me." But then it circles back to the two biggies.

There's just something inherently karaokelike about the '80s musical style—the overproduced drums, the beer-commercial sax solos, the keytars, the leather-lung vocal melodrama. Eighties songs do not belong to the singer, not the way a James Taylor or Stevie Wonder song does. They don't sound like a person expressing a feeling—they sound like a gigantic sound machine blowing up this feeling to self-parodic heights. For some people, that's a reason to dislike '80s music, but for me, overstatement was part of the fun. Eighties songs sound like they're karaoke already.

I never sang karaoke in the '80s, but I spend my karaoke time rehearsing those years, long after the audition ended. I go to karaoke to live those years out in ways that weren't possible at the time, technologically or emotionally. Now I can step into the stilettos of Sheena or Chaka. These are songs I used to sing alone in my room—now I have a microphone and a crowd.

Sometimes karaoke lets you go back to the memories attached to the song. When Ally sings with her friend Marisa, they are the only two people in the room. They were BFFs in high school because they both had U2 stickers on their lockers. They used to sing each other the Nirvana song "Drain You" and pretend they were the two babies in the song. They have been through countless adventures together that they'll never tell their husbands about, except via karaoke.

Whenever they sing George Michael, they giggle. There's definitely a story there I'm not in on.

The mike has lots of echo and delay, so even if you can't hit any actual notes (like me) you can fake it. There's something '80s about that too. Karaoke is the show—if you impersonate INXS for a few minutes and it doesn't feel right, you don't have to take them home with you.

One night, going through all the Boy George songs in the book, Ally sang "The Crying Game." It's a song I can't endure because it makes me sad—everybody has those. Sad songs are like the bartenders in the old black-and-white detective movies. They provide a sympathetic ear. But they spend enough time listening to people cry and complain. Sometimes you have to put the song away for a while, just to give it a break. Like in the movie *Don't Bother to Knock* where Richard Widmark is the tough guy at the bar, drinking bourbon and grousing about the ladies. He doesn't believe in settling down. "Get married, become a statistic."

"Yeah," the bartender replies. "Stay single, and you wind up talking to bartenders."

"The Crying Game" is a bartender I've spent too much time talking to, so I had to put the song away forever and figured I'd never be able to hear it again. I gave up trying to listen to it years ago—but she brings it back to life for me. Sometimes karaoke also lets you escape the memories and hear the song fresh. If a song is too painful, to play at home, you use the karaoke room as a safe place to try it on again.

I never knew karaoke existed until the early '90s, when Charlottesville got a bar called Mingles. Like every Southern karaoke joint, it had an Elvis Guy who sat by himself at the bar, waiting for his turn. He always does "The American Trilogy," ending with his fist in the air as he cries, "His truth is marching on!" Then he sits down by himself. Other people do Elvis songs, but nobody tops the Elvis Guy. Some things are meant to be.

It wasn't until I was well into my thirties when I was at a bleak point in my life, a depressed widower who found ordinary social interactions painful, that I first sang karaoke. It was so much easier to sing than to talk. When I found out that I had other friends who liked to sing, it became an obsession. Suddenly, this was social interaction. I met my friend Laura one night because I was doing "Young Americans" and she decided to grab the mike and be the backup chorus. Needless to say, we've been friends ever since.

Laura bemoans the fact that karaoke is not more like real life. She asks, "Why do I have all the confidence in karaoke that's completely missing from any other area of my existence?" I wonder the same thing.

I first experienced the private room in early 2001, one night when we got tired of waiting around some East Village dump for our songs to get called. Nils and Jennie whisked me off to Koreatown. We spent the night in a shiny room where every flat surface was covered with mirrors. It was like a Robert Downey Jr. movie, with the same soundtrack but only one drug: karaoke. They gave me an overnight crash course in commanding the microphone and surrendering to the song. We subjected one another to selections ranging from the undeniable ("Lovergirl") to the unsingable ("Word Up") to the physical ("Physical"). When we straggled out to the sidewalk at ten the next morning, already late for work, we joked about how sordid we must have looked, rubbing our eyes at the sun like teen runaways in an Aerosmith video. But I felt like a new man, even if the new man felt like Cyndi Lauper wobbling home in the morning light. Karaoke, like money, changes everything.

Ally is bouncing on the couch now, doing "Going Back to Cali." Asif and Jennie missed it when she sang it before, because they were out having a smoke, so they demanded it again. Nobody minds going back. "To Cali, Cali, Cali!" Ally chants. "Yo, I don't think so!" I missed it before when she sang the Cure's "Fascination Street," but I won't make her sing it again. You can always go back later. There are more songs that need to be heard right now.

At Sing Sing, they kick us out at four. There's always some melancholy when it comes time to punch in the final songs of the night. Everybody picks their last song, and then, inevitably, someone notices something else in the songbook that didn't catch their eye before. Okay, one more.

A group sing? No, not "We Are the World." It seems like a good idea but it's always a mistake. No Michael Jackson—too sad, too soon. It looks like Chaka Khan is getting a little more action tonight. When it's a toss-up between Chaka Khan and Sheena Easton, Chaka wins three times out of five. This time Ally's doing the rap, Caryn is doing the Chaka part, and the rest of us are just going to feel it.

PRINCE

"Purple Rain"

1984

I was the ice cream man the summer after high school. It was the perfect job—driving eighteen hours a day, just me, the streets of Boston, my tunes and my truck, hustling a freezer full of toxic chocolate sludge. Every morning, I stocked up in Charlestown and hit the road, pimping my Nutty Buddies, Hoodsies, Bomb Pops and Gobstoppers block to block. This was the best job ever. I had visions of lissome brunettes pulling crisply folded twenties out of their bikini tops with the command, "Cool me off, sugar boy."

Instead, these visions gave way to a reality of sitting in Southeast Expressway traffic all day, munching ice cream sandwiches, slurping Mountain Dew, singing along to the radio, all to bring the Chipwiches and Chocolate Whirls to the sweaty little children of my town. There hadn't been an ice cream man in town for years—the previous guy had blown his license by selling weed out of his truck. So I was bringing ice cream to blocks that were starved for it.

I pushed all kinds of weight: popsicles, Fudgsicles, dreamsicles, Creamsicles. Take a ride on the white line highway, my white lines go a long way. Pay the toll, sell your soul, my Nutty Buddy's nice and cold. Since I was paying wholesale for a truckload of them, and I was my own boss, I could eat into the profits all I wanted. With all due respect to Tony Montana in *Scarface*, my policy was to get high on my own supply.

To this day, when I hear "Purple Rain," I can taste the La Dip—a revolting concoction consisting of two deep-fried chocolate chip cookies, the kind you'd get out of a hospital vending machine, with a block of vanilla ice cream in between, and then the whole shebang given an inch-thick coat of fudge and then apparently battered in some strange kind of sucrose tempura. It was like a hockey puck, except harder to digest. Every time I chomped away on one, I wondered, what kind of God permits such a thing to exist? A fucking righteous God.

I vowed on my first day that girls who flirted with the ice cream man would get free La Dips. This didn't turn out to be the profit drain I anticipated.

I leased the truck from the Universal Ice Cream Company in Boston, and bought the ice cream, candy, bubble gum, soda, etc., wholesale from them. I did not mess around with soft serve, which is a whole other genre of ice cream man. Every morning,

I drove into the warehouse and took a few minutes to fill out the order form. Let's see. Nobody wants Toffee Krunch Bars, delicious though they might be. Screwball Orange? Too complex for the masses. Malt Cup? Too subtle. Chunka Choklit? Now we're talking. Freeze Pops? On the money! Astro Pops? On lots and lots of money!

The guys at the Universal Ice Cream Company were a mysterious bunch. I liked to imagine they were shady underworld characters, but they were probably just badly dressed. Randy, the owner and boss, was a great guy, walking around the warehouse with a clipboard that had nothing attached to it. He wore a Members Only jacket (it was cold inside that place) and shades, hairy as a panda. For some reason, the boss would always greet me with a Greek joke. Did he think I was Greek? I don't recall how it came up, but without fail, every morning, he would grab my hand and say something like, "What's virgin wool in Argos?" or "What's the motto of the Spartan army?"

"Hey duuude, how you doing?" I would reply. The word "dude" was brand-new on the East Coast that summer, and if it's now hard to imagine life without it, that's mainly because it functions so efficiently as a way of acknowledging someone's physical presence while discreetly backing away. The word could be stretched into one long vowel while you inched closer to the door, and it was easier than laughing at Randy's jokes.

Randy was a big Springsteen fan—who wasn't that summer? As a result, whenever you handed in your order for Dubble Bubble, he would sing, "This gum's for hiii-yaaah!"

The first time I drove in to beg for the job, he sat me down and told me about the last guy. "Goddamn hippie," he said. "Sold the drugs right out of the truck. You're not on the drugs, are you?"

"No way, dude," I said. "What this world is coming to."

"You're gonna have to go in and interview for the license, and the first thing they're going to do is look in your eyes. You know why?"

"Why?"

"Because they can see the drugs in your eyes."

"Awesome."

"You look like a nice kid," he said, touching his shades yet not budging them a bit, just hinting at the existence of shades-removal as a conversational gambit. "But if I ever hear about you selling anything, I will break your goddamn ankles."

"Got it."

"Ever drive a truck before?"

"No."

"Good. Hey, how did Socrates separate the men from the boys?"

I got the license. I did not sell the drugs. I had my route all mapped out—Jamaica Plain, West Roxbury, Hyde Park and Milton, miles and miles of hungry kids. If I started early in the morning, I could make the whole route in eighteen hours, get back to Charlestown, and plug in the truck so the freezer could recharge overnight. The next morning, I'd be right back on the road. Ice cream sleeps for no man.

My truck had a big green dragon painted on the door, to

show the customers where you stick the trash. The dragon's mouth cleverly surrounded the hole in the door where the garbage bag went. If I punched the button on the dashboard, I could turn on the revolving lights up front, to let all passersby know that ice cream was rolling through. There was also a button to ring the bell. And *no*, it was not one of those newfangled ice cream trucks that plays a stupid jingle all the time. No, no, no. I hear those all the time in my neighborhood now and I shake my head. These trucks offend my professional code. You know what that means? It means he *doesn't respect the ice cream*. A real ice cream man doesn't play a little jingle—just a bell that rings and says "never fear, the ice cream man is here, let's see those dimes and quarters appear" without hassling people with a jingle.

I see the ice cream man on my block, and he makes the kids wait in line. You know what that means? That's right, you heard me—it means he *doesn't respect the ice cream*. It also means he probably sells the drugs.

Like playing a stupid jingle—you betray the whole experience when you make people stand in line. The kids want to crowd around the ice cream truck and look inside, ogle all the flavors and freezers, like boozers standing at the bar. Nobody wants to be put on the spot, forced to make up their mind fast like they're standing at the free-throw line. Of course, people want to feel like they're waiting their turn, without others cutting in line ahead of them, but a real ice cream man knows how to reassure the customers that he remembers whose turn is when. You're here to make people relax, enjoy the presence of the truck, not make it a stressful experience. You're here to respect the ice cream. Can't sell it without insulting it? Fine. Somebody else will, buddy.

This was the best job I ever had, even if it meant putting up with little kids all day. I learned a lot about crowd control. Sno-Cones were the toughest. You have to open them for the kid, because they're basically a fat chunk of ice in a plastic bag. Two out of three Sno-Cones get dumped on the ground while the kid is trying to rip them open. I think they must design them that way on purpose. So when you give a kid a Sno-Cone, you better have a back-up handy. After the first Sno-Cone hits the dirt, you have to hustle the new one into their hands pronto. You have a two- or three-second window.

They never cry right away. They always stare at the ground in shock, then fast-forward through denial, anger, depression and acceptance before they start to wail. This is the worst thing that's ever happened to them. That Sno-Cone on the sidewalk is the end of innocence, the first lesson that the world is out to nail them, and you do *not* want to be there when this happens.

The kid is crushed. The other kids stare at you in Sno-Conenfreude. The parents are pissed. You have to get the new Sno-Cone into their mitts *before* they start crying, or it's too late.

Everybody was always glad to see me. Who doesn't love the ice cream man? The kids turned out to be plenty of fun. They were, in a manner of speaking, my kids. I kept them cool. By the end of June, the shorties on the route knew when to show up. They knew to stay on the sidewalk until the truck stopped, because they knew an ice cream man puts child safety first. They knew not to ask the ice cream man annoying questions like "Do you have a girlfriend?"

"Hey ice cream man, how much money do they pay you?"

"Simmer down, you rascals. I don't do this for money. I do it for the love of ice cream."

"Do you sleep in the truck?"

"Do you got a bathroom in the truck?"

"You got any Lotsa Fizz?"

"Yes, my young whippersnapper with the arcane taste. I ordered some just for you."

"Hey ice cream man, do you got a girlfriend?"

"Right bitches. Who wants a Bomb Pop?"

Nobody wanted a Bomb Pop. They were easily the most worthless crap in the truck. Red, white and blue lacrosse sticks made of ice, completely flavorless, barely worth the room they took up in the freezer. I priced them at a dime, in case any absolute bottom feeders wanted the cheapest item I had, but really, you'd be better off sucking on the dime. Moreover, Bomb Pops were possessed of dubious patriotic overtones.

"Hey, Randy, I'm not sure about these Bomb Pops."

"Kids *love* the Bomb Pops. What are you talking about? Need a fresh case?"

"Dude, it's gonna take me all summer to unload the ones you already sold me."

"There's no such thing as bad ice cream. Only a bad ice cream man."

"It isn't really even ice cream, though. More like ice. Besides, don't you think the name is a bit obnoxious?"

"What? It's a bomb of ice cream. *Ka-boom!*"

"I don't know, dude. As a draft-age male, I wonder if you've considered the nausea that the words 'bomb pop' evoke in your late-adolescent customers. Don't you think the threat of thermonuclear war vitiates the innocent pleasures of summer refreshments?"

"Ah, get out of here, kid. It's always been called the Bomb Pop, and it always will be. Red, white and blue."

Randy was proud of the Bomb Pop name. He had a framed letter on his office wall from Congressman Ed Markey, who used to drive for the Universal Ice Cream Company to work his way through law school. The letter jovially suggested they change "Bomb Pop" to something less morbid, like the "Nuclear Freeze." Randy wouldn't budge.

"Fine. Maybe I'll sell one to Caspar Weinberger."

"Cheer up, kid. Hey, did I tell you about the Greek tampon? It's called 'Abzorba the Leak.'"

I had push-ups, which would have intrigued me more if I'd known that push-up bras even existed, but unfortunately my knowledge of women's underwear was a little rudimentary at the time. I had chocolate eclairs, Snickers bars, cans of soda that only cost me a dime apiece, which meant they were practically free, and the good old ice cream sandwich, which only cost me a nickel. There was hardly anything I sold that I didn't eat in any imaginable combination. I was self-employed, so I could pull over any time I wanted and gorge my face full of frosty atrocities. I would roll over to my parents' house for lunch and ply my sisters with goodies. All I asked my sisters in return was that they say, "You are wise and generous, oh ice cream man."

I kept my Walkman on the dashboard, plugged into a couple of speakers from Bradlee's. I played the radio, which was full of great shit that summer. It was a historic summer for Top 40 radio, as anyone who lived through it will tell you. The country was in terrible shape, nuclear war was just around the corner, movies sucked, TV sucked and the Red Sox had just traded Dennis Eckersley for Bill Buckner—but pop was on a roll, and the most advanced music being created anywhere in the world was right there crackling out of my cheapshit speakers.

I was eighteen, and I liked both kinds of music: Echo *and* the Bunnymen. But Top 40 was so rich that every damn station on the dial was playing something incredible. I loved to crank up the volume in the Callahan Tunnel, where you can literally hear the music bounce off the walls. When you have Prince on the radio, all the ice cream you can gobble in the freezer and nothing to do but drive a truck in Boston traffic without a single lesson on how, being eighteen is pretty close to bearable.

I lived on ice cream sandwiches and Top 40 hits all summer, dodging traffic on the Southeast Expressway singing along to an endless loop of "Purple Rain" and "99 Luftballons" and "Roxanne Roxanne" and "Ghostbusters" and "Girls Just Want to Have Fun" and "Missing You." I heard Bruce Springsteen's "Dancing in the Dark" so many times a day, I translated it into Spanish just for sheer psychic self-preservation. (*"¡No haces fuego! ¡No haces in fuego en la soledad! ¡Estoy bailando, bailando por la oscuridad!")* And every time Prince strummed that cathedral-sized opening guitar chord of "Purple Rain," it felt like the ice cream truck was a spaceship lifting off to bring Creamsicles to distant constellations—even when I was stuck in traffic on Storrow Drive.

My favorite kids were at the corner of Highland and Herman in Dorchester, where I'd arrive around nine. Stacey, Manny and Pepito would breakdance for free ice cream, singing songs like "Centipede" and "Cool It Now." I would park, eat my dinner of La Dips and Orange Crush, and reflect on a day's work well done, giving these kids whatever I felt like getting rid of. Then they would make me hide behind the door and make painful noises, so they could throw rocks at the dragon and make him roar.

"Hey ice cream man, the dragon is in pain!"

"That dragon is hurting!"

"Die, dragon!"

"Hey, ice cream man, you got a girlfriend?"

The kids at High Point Village in West Roxbury were special because they were allowed to sass the ice cream man. This was a privilege rarely extended. They called me "R.E.M.," because that was the music they heard coming out of my truck one afternoon. They thought it was incredibly funny to meet a guy who actually listened to R.E.M., and they did mean imitations of the singer Michael Stipe in the video, clutching earphones and wailing, "I'm soooorryyyyy! I'm soooorryyyyy!"

"Hey, R.E.M., do you live in the truck?"

"Do you got a girl in the truck?"

"A naked girl?"

"Hey, R.E.M., do you sell any dimebags, man?"

"Gimme something free, R.E.M.!"

Nobody else was allowed to sass me.

I would sell to girls around town I had crushes on, girls whose communions at St. Mary's I had gazed upon as an altar boy, now girls who bought ice cream from me. It would have been nice if any of these girls had noticed me. It would have been even nicer if they'd said, "Excuse me, Mr. Ice Cream Eye Candy, but I'm having trouble getting my tongue warmed up—could you spare a girl some practice licks? I don't know, I guess I'm feeling a little . . . *fros-tay!*"

This never happened.

On weekends, I parked by the Public Garden, or near the Boston Tea Party Ship. I sat in the truck and read Kafka's *The Trial* or some depressive shit like that, waiting for tourists. I snickered at English people for calling popsicles "ice lollies." On the Fourth of July, my friend Barak and I parked the truck by the Esplanade for the Boston Pops concert and made an absolute killing. On the way home, traffic was backed up so far that people were getting out of their cars to come buy something, or passing bills from car to car. By the end of the night, we were tossing free ice cream cones out the window, since we'd bought more than we could store in the freezer. God bless America. (Nobody bought any Bomb Pops, however.)

To tell the truth, I was a little bit drunk on my new popularity. Nobody wanted to antagonize the ice cream man, because they knew I would never stop on their street again. So I was treated like a visiting king. It's fair to say I lost perspective. I began referring to myself in the third person, even when I was mumbling to myself in the truck, saying things like "The ice cream man will now stop for lunch," or "The ice cream man could use another Hoodsie." Even driving my crappy old Chevy Nova home, I would announce, "The ice cream man is signaling to switch to the left lane. Stand back lest ye melt!" My sisters began grumbling and calling me Snow Miser.

It was the closest I'd ever come to being a star, the kind that Prince was in *Purple Rain*, riding that motorcycle around with Apollonia on the back, cruising Lake Minnetonka, suffering the hard work of being so beautiful that people bombard you with attention day and night. I was already a big fan, but watching *Purple Rain*, I thought, this is my life. Finally, someone else gets it. I felt like Prince could understand what I was going through. We'd have to hang out some time. He could play me some tasty new tracks, and maybe I could serve him a Hoodsie.

PAUL McCARTNEY

"No More Lonely Nights"

1984

It was Paul McCartney who warped my young brain with the idea that not worshipping a girl was a waste of time, an idea that has caused about 88 percent of the misery in my life. (The other 12 percent was caused by "Say Say Say.")

Paul McCartney is one of the central mysteries of my universe. He's the only Beatle people really argue about. The other three, for better or worse, are fixed in their roles—John as the caustic rebel, George as the religious one, Ringo as the drummer. But Paul is the loose cannon, the danger Beatle, the X in the fab equation. He's the only one you can mention in a bar to start an argument. Nobody really knows what to do with Paul, which is why I think about him all the time.

Paul was the bitchiest Beatle. Everybody knows the other Beatles thought he was bossy. Even in the interviews for the 1990s *Anthology* documentaries, George Harrison physically bristles in his company. But he was the Beatle who worked hardest, who forced the others to finish their songs and show up to the studio.

Paul is the bossy Irish sister in the Beatles. Every Irish family has one of these, and it's always the oldest girl. My cousin Graine in Dublin explained to me that this sister is called "the Alsatian," which is the British Isles term for the breed of dog that Americans call a Doberman. "I'm the Alsatian in my family," she explained at one family dinner. We were standing against a wall watching our cousins congregate from all over Ireland, noting the uncanny pattern—every family seemed to have a gang of sisters. "Yes, but there's only one of *us* per family," she told me. "The Alsatian—the enforcer. I'm the one who stirs the pot and speaks my mind. I'm the Alsatian in my family. Ann is the Alsatian in yours."

Any Irish brother can recognize what Paul was doing in the Beatles. He was the Alsatian. He kept coming up with more work for them to do, dreaming up big, daft ideas, sometimes brilliant (*Sgt. Pepper, Abbey Road*), sometimes involving walrus costumes (*Magical Mystery Tour*). He got mad if he didn't think they were pushing hard enough. It always cracks me up that some people describe "Getting Better" as a cheerful, optimistic song. Nagging the other Beatles about how things could be better, a little better, all the fucking time—that sounds like Paul to me.

Paul was the girliest Beatle, the prettiest star with the long eyelashes. He was one of the original rock-and-roll gender-benders, which is why he was the most new-wave Beatle. But if his prettiness helped create the Beatles, it was his bitchiness that kept them alive, and it isn't much of an exaggeration to say that the Beatles were his fantasy—every time the others were burned out and felt like trying something different, not being Beatles anymore, it was Paul who would herd them back into the group. John dismissed his tunes as "granny music." Exactly—I bet Paul's granny was one tough Irish broad who could beat up any bartender in Liverpool. And I also bet she had some terrified brothers.

That's why he still bugs people. His image might be the pop softie, the one who blows kisses to the old ladies, the one who plays it safe. But paradoxically, he's the only Beatle that people despise. Beatles histories tend to agree about everything *except* the Paul Question, which is where they get contentious. Countless bands have styled themselves in opposition to the Beatles, as the "bad boys" of rock: the Stones, Led Zeppelin, the Sex Pistols, etc. These bands set out to piss people off. But there's no way they could possibly piss people off the way Paul does.

Paul's girl worship will always be the most disturbing and mysterious thing about him. It is strange, no matter how you look at it, that he likes them so much, considering the time and place when he became a rock star. He waltzed into a life where, by the time he was twenty-two, he knew for a fact that no whim would ever be refused him, whether it was sex, drugs, cars, gurus or druids. (Football teams—I think lots of English rock stars buy those.) Paul chose to be a husband. In nearly thirty years together, he and

Linda famously never spent a night apart, except when he was in jail for smuggling weed into Tokyo.

The Stones suggested that if you dabble in decadence, you could turn into a devil-worshipping junkie. Paul McCartney suggested that if you mess around with girl worship, you could turn into a husband. So Paul was a lot scarier.

He didn't just sing about the way love messes up your mind—he lived it out. He even let his wife, Linda, join the band. Everybody made fun of him for that; everybody knew the joke, "What do you call a dog with wings?" There's no way Paul didn't know the whole world was laughing at him for giving his wife so much of his attention—he just didn't care. Or maybe he did it to annoy people. (And it is both weird and impossible not to notice that all four Beatles had absurdly long-lived marriages, second marriages in most of their cases—did any other major rock band spawn such notoriously doting husbands?)

Paul has been called many things—sappy, sentimental, complacent, a pothead, a mama's boy, dead, the Walrus. But never a misogynist, which definitely makes him stand out from the other rock stars of his generation. As early as 1968, the first biographer to write a book about the Beatles, Hunter Davies, noted that Paul was the one with "modern" attitudes about women. (He compared some of the others to Andy Capp.) Even before he married Linda, he was squiring the actress Jane Asher, making him one of very few '60s rock stars whose choice of female companion was another creative artist. He was always vocal in giving her credit for helping to introduce him to things like classical music and modern art, the things that influenced Beatles albums like *Sgt. Pepper* and *Revolver*. And he fawned on Linda, so he spent the *Boogie Nights* era on an organic farm in Scotland, raising four kids and eating her steamed wheatgrass casseroles.

In his music, even from his earliest days, Paul liked girls so much that he sounded phony when he tried to be mean. The only time he ever sang an "it ain't me babe" song, he came up with "Another Girl," which is laughably insincere. And even then he disses one chick because he met another who "will always be my friend." He became insanely famous by singing about how he liked girls, but once he got famous, he just seemed to go right on liking them.

You have to admit, there aren't many stories like Paul Mc-Cartney's in the annals of rock and roll, or showbiz in general. This was the most ardently desired male on earth, not to mention one of Britain's top earners. Most of us would not have made the sexual choices he made, given his options. I have no idea how he treated his groupies in the '60s—although maybe it has to signify something that none of them ever sold him out to the tabloids. But if it was ever a pain in the ass to be married to Linda, who by all accounts was as tough-minded and stubborn as he was, the world never heard about it. And when John and Yoko split up in the early 1970s, guess who Yoko sent to L.A. to go talk to John?

People have spent many years trying to figure out what happened to Paul McCartney, but maybe we're not really asking the right questions. His flaws are actually not that hard to figure out. ("Maybe he used to smoke dope every waking moment" explains a lot of them.) It's his virtues that seem profoundly fucked up. He was a man deranged by love, driven to madness by a happy love affair, a deeper madness than other rock stars got from their unhappy ones. By the late 1970s, most of his peers were making their divorce albums, but McCartney was knocking out increasingly crazed nondivorce albums, and nobody ever enjoyed being a husband more than this man. "Maybe I'm Amazed" is an infinitely freakier song than "Revolution Number 9." Linda seemed like nobody's idea of an obsession-worthy muse, just some random hippie chick Paul liked. It would have been one thing if he'd married Elizabeth Taylor or Jackie Kennedy. But he married a photographer who did the album cover art for Tommy James and the Shondells.

I'm not claiming to like all the music—far from it. "Let 'Em In" is some kind of high-bongwater mark for how zonked and sedated a grown man can sound when things are going too smoothly. Songs like this terrify me. I mean, Keith Richards has some impressive vices, and I always love hearing gossip about them. But they only disturb me in theory. In real life, I'm not in any danger of turning into Keith Richards, and neither are my friends.

But turning into Paul McCartney? It could happen to *anybody*. Some of your friends are probably already this fucked.

Two of my friends have met him, neither one affiliated with the music biz or the media in any way, and both used the same word to describe him. I hate admitting that the word was "dumb," and I hate recalling I was unreasonably aggressive both times in defending him. But I know what they mean. A lot of smart people think Paul McCartney is dumb, and it's easy to see why. He doesn't worry about looking cool. He doesn't have the defensive armor we expect in people who have been visible all their lives. Like a lot of naturally intense people, he seems to have overcompensated with an almost cartoonishly easygoing manner. His moronic public actions get more attention than his smart ones. I mean, there are great songs on his recent albums, but who the hell listens to them? Nobody. Meanwhile, millions of people around the world watched the Super Bowl when Macca showed up and sang an impromptu duet with Terry Bradshaw of "A Hard Day's Night."

Indeed, his flaws are a nonstop source of comic delight. He has no apparent ability to feel shame. If Terry Bradshaw wants to sing, Paul's game. If he wants to release hit singles so cringingly awful I would rather gnaw off my fingers than type the titles, he goes for it. He sponsored an authorized biography where he detailed how much harder he worked than the other Beatles—he wrote 65 percent of this song, 70 percent of that song. Somebody really should have talked him out of that. Also, during the period he was married to the unspeakable Heather Mills, the *Give My Regards to Broad Street* of Beatle wives, she was clearly goading him into being more of a bitch than he normally is, telling him she'd never heard of songs like "Get Back." (You're married to Paul McCartney! Google the man!) That was when Paul began his deeply embarrassing campaign to change the songwriting credit from Lennon-McCartney to McCartney-Lennon.

When he divorced this nightmare of a second wife, her lawyers claimed that, among other cruelties, Paul had gotten angry at her for breastfeeding, allegedly telling her, "They are *my* breasts!" I love that story. Yeah, right—Paul raised his kids on an organic farm with the crunchiest hippie mama who ever lived, so I suspect he was familiar with the concept of nursing. The lawyers should have tried something believable, like "He fell asleep and left the baby on the plane" or "He wrote 'Say Say Say.'"

Of course, anyone can sympathize with the other Beatles. If you're George, and you wrote a great song like "Taxman," you have every reason to be furious that Paul dubbed his guitar solo over yours. But so what? Paul just played it better. Paul didn't even care about claiming the credit—99 percent of listeners assume George played the "Taxman" solo, and apparently that's always been fine with Paul. (I had no idea until a few years ago, when the Beatles' engineer Geoff Emerick revealed it in his book *Here, There and Everywhere*.) He let George take the credit; all he wanted was to play the damn thing. "Let It Be"? Not really his style.

Paul was the Beatle who was never embarrassed about having been a Beatle. He spent his Hall of Fame induction speech urging them to induct George and Ringo. When he was knighted, he said, "It's strange being here without the other three." He's bewilderingly generous to the idea of the group, and one could say it's because he tended to get his way in that group, but considering the decades of success he had without them, his deference to the others is a bit baffling.

Nothing, however, can explain how he convinced a capitalist record label to release *Give My Regards to Broad Street*, which gave the world "No More Lonely Nights." I only know this record because I bought it as a Christmas present for Ann in 1984. We listened in awe. This album is mostly composed of orchestral remakes of Beatles songs, fluffed up by Paul in the nadir of his tragic Hawaiian shirt phase. It has "No More Lonely Nights," which is a surprisingly gorgeous tune, and deserves to be remembered as an '80s pop trifle on par with the best of Phil Collins or Steve Perry. Yet it's completely forgotten because it was buried on the soundtrack of this infamously ass movie. Not even Ann, a confirmed Paulmaniac, could find anything nice to say about this album.

Paul really only makes sense to me as an Irish big sister. His loyalty to the group is second only to that of my sister Ann, who would take a bullet or even two for any of her siblings, yet would not think of letting us board a plane without drawing up a diagram of how we should pack our suitcases. She works harder than we do.

Ann is a take-charge gal. Ann is the only one of us who can drive a stick, the one you'd call from a Turkish prison to explain you'd be late for dinner. When one of our basements gets flooded, Ann is the one who drives over with the sump pump before being asked. Ann taught our ninety-year-old grandfather to use the microwave, knowing full well he'd never touch it. She organized my mom's closets and wanted to throw everything away; my mom insisted on keeping our first-communion blankets. They argued over this for days. Ann finally said, "Fine. When you're gone, they're gone."

My mom likes to say that Caroline is her daughter, Tracey is her sister, and Ann is her mother. I am old enough to remember my mom and her mom having the same arguments that Mom and Ann have now, usually involving one telling the other what to do.

Ann is the girl my grandmother warned me about, because she is the girl my grandmother was. My grandfather used to call her "the girl from Glenbeigh," because she looks just like her. Nana knew this was coming. Back in County Kerry, she was Bridget Courtney, and she continued to terrify her brothers even after she had crossed the ocean and settled in the new world. Nana was "fussy," as she herself put it. She was fond of giving orders on behalf of her grandson, mostly the matter of who was going to feed him in the immediate future, so I had no complaints. But the point is, you want this woman on your side. If somebody is invading your country or the river is flooding your farm, the Alsatian is who you want on your team. Or, if you're one of the Beatles, you want Paul in your band.

When my grandfather tried explaining the Alsatian to me, he said it was the Courtney temper versus the Twomey temper. My grandfather, my sisters and my mom got the Courtney temper, where you blow your top and then it's over. He and I got the Twomey temper, where you stew about it for hours and hope it goes away. He told me it was better for everyone to have the Courtney version, and apologized for passing on the wrong kind to me. I didn't mind that—I was grateful to be surrounded by all these women. All I wanted to know was how to live with them in peace.

I'm sure he would have told me, if he had any idea.

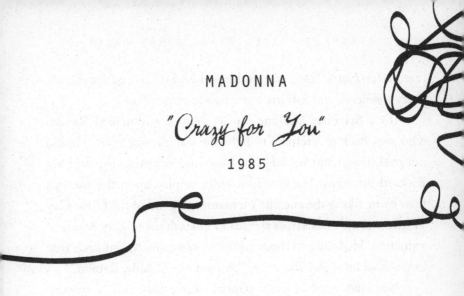

MADONNA

"Crazy for You"
1985

In general, people do not remember 1985. It's the decade's forgotten year, even when people have made their peace with the rest of the '80s on so many levels. At this point, everybody admits that the early '80s new-wave stars were the bomb, and late '80s hip-hop and disco stars were tubular. But 1985? It was the year of the great awesomeness drought.

The reason, obviously, can be summed up in one word: *Rambo.* If you were alive at the time, this name probably brings back a Proustian rush of memory, but if you're too young to remember, *Rambo* was a hit movie in 1985, a year so starved for laughs that Rambo became the big summer blockbuster. And it gives us traumatic post-disorder stress trauma or whatever it was Rambo suffered after 'Nam. There was nothing else to do but go see *Rambo* every weekend, and it hurts too much to remember.

It's a Sylvester Stallone movie about a guy named Rambo who goes back to Vietnam to fight the war all over again. He did not pack a shirt, but he did bring bows and arrows and a nice little Richard Simmons headband, in order to play upon the enemy's fears by invoking the ancient Vietnamese legend of the Great Gay Warrior who comes across the sea to unleash his mighty power of seduction. He kills everybody in the whole country, and finds true love with a local girl who says, "You not expendable, Rambo."

No matter what your politics were, this was a spleen-punchingly funny movie and everybody went to see it six times. If you weren't born at the time, you have never heard of this movie, even though every other Vietnam franchise is in constant week-end TV rotation, from *Delta Force* to *Missing in Action*, as is every other Stallone movie from *Rocky* to *Demolition Man*. *Rambo*'s been written out of history. But in 1985, it was a brilliant movie to watch in the theater, especially if everybody in the crowd was high as a kite. The third time I went, as they rolled the credits, the guy behind me told his buddies, "I got a fuckin' woody already!"

However, it sucked and nobody remembered it a year later, because nobody liked to think we were all so desperate. So 1985 is the memory gap no one wants to recall, much like the way Willis and Arnold on *Diff'rent Strokes* blocked out their traumatic memories of 1975 (inspiring the shocking "Willis throws book at annoying tutor who won't shut up about 1975" episode).

The only other thing we did for fun in 1985 is talk shit about

Madonna and how much we hated her and how we couldn't wait for her to go away. Except she didn't.

Madonna entered my life with the "Burning Up" video, which was so sexy it just made me mad. She turned my private Catholic angst into a spectacle, a one-woman Vatican 3. "What's a-matter?" she asked in the "Open Your Heart" twelve-inch remix. "You scared a-me or something?" Well, yes.

I couldn't believe anybody could be as brazen as she was. What the movie said about Rambo was truer about Madonna: "What you call hell, she calls home." I was a shy boy who craved a not-shy girl to be Madonna for me. She dared me to open my heart, and now I had to figure out how, listening to her for clues. I was lost in Madonnadolatry. And I was pissed off about it.

Of all the complex females in my life, Madonna was the one who taught me how to be completely exasperated by a woman, and how to like it. She was the first woman who ever told me I can dance (I can't) and the first who told me I came when she wished for me (I'll have to take her word on that one). I literally never go the movies without thinking about the scene in the "Into the Groove" video where she puts her head on the guy's shoulder and lets him feed her popcorn. She screwed me up good. Oh, Madonna—you put this in me, so now what? So now what?

By now she's saturated popular music longer than anyone else from that time. For me, it's "Angel," "Who's That Girl," "Keep It Together," "Bad Girl." For you, it might be "Papa Don't Preach" or "Deeper and Deeper" or "Frozen" (none of which ever did it for me, but you never know).

Some of her songs are so beautiful it hurts to feel them pierce my body, making me too sad to listen to them ("What It Feels Like for a Girl," "Promise to Try"). Some make me happy every time, like "Dress You Up"—that *thwamp-thwamp-thwamp* synth-snare intro, exactly one second long, and exactly as perfect as any number of equally joyous seconds in that song. Some become my go-to karaoke jams ("Crazy for You" on a vodka night, "Justify My Love" for bourbon), some evoke deep historical paradoxes ("Angel" is the same song as both Lou Reed's "Crazy Feeling" and the Stylistics' "Betcha By Golly, Wow"—how the hell did that happen?), sometimes she sounds silly enunciating the consonants ("Drowned World/Substitute for Love"), sometimes she gasps for breath between low notes she can't hit ("Angel"). Sometimes she says "Whee!" and sometimes she says "Hey!" As a cruel Italian goddess, she does stupid things like *Evita* or the "Secret" video, but that's just her painful way of teaching us not to trust her.

One of the reasons I keep listening to her, whether I want to or not, is that she keeps teaching me about how difficult women are, how needy and pushy they are, how silly it is to think you can control them or make them what you want them to be. I guess I should have learned this lesson years ago, but I never do, so I keep getting burned by Madonna. I guess that's one of the reasons I keep her around.

In 1985, it was still possible to believe Madonna was just a flash in the pan. She was this year's girl. I was a librarian that summer, shelving books to the radio. Every time a Madonna song came on, my coworkers, groovy lesbians with new-wave haircuts, raved about how Madonna was the shit. This made me feel a little stupid. And so did the yearning in Madonna's voice when she hits those growly low notes in "Crazy for You."

At nineteen, I had never had a girlfriend, and I knew for a fact that this was somebody's fault, though not mine. So I decided it was Madonna's. I had pretty strict ideas about how I thought the world should be, and my plan for getting a girlfriend was to make the world rearrange itself to conform to my conditions. I thought that was a fair set of demands. Madonna kept reminding me, over and over, how full of shit I was. So I resented her bitterly and prayed for her to not be famous anymore. I was sure she was going to have a short run anyway.

In August, my parents took me and my sisters on a road trip through Europe. Four of us were packed in the backseat cruising through Spain, Italy and France. So it was a summer spent in the car with my sisters, like so many summers and so many family road trips. We sat in the backseat and sang every song we knew, from "American Pie" to the *Joseph and the Amazing Technicolor Dreamcoat* soundtrack. Ann and Caroline sang every song on Ronnie Milsap's greatest hits, just to annoy me and Tracey.

The book I brought with me was Virginia Woolf's *Mrs. Dalloway*, a gift from a girl I liked, except I read her inscription even more obsessively than the novel. "For you," she wrote inside the front cover. "Read this and think of me. This pen is horrible." The ink ran dry halfway through "horrible," leaving me with questions. "For you"? What did that mean? Why didn't she pick a new pen to write the rest of the inscription, so she could sign her name and maybe add some hearts or "XOXO"s? It was a mystery. I loved the novel but I had to admit, my concentration kept wandering back to that girl's handwriting.

We had a radio in the car, but we rarely turned it on because the songs were all Madonna, as they were back in the States.

We all had destinations we were keen to see—Ann was looking forward to Rome, Tracey to Milan, Caroline to the ruins of Pompeii. But I was waiting for Lourdes, the sacred Catholic shrine in the French countryside. I was nineteen and extremely devout, struggling with all my screwed-up obsessions about Catholicism—and, as was inevitable, they were all tangled up in my screwed-up obsessions about Madonna.

Religion was something I'd been somewhat cuckoo about all through my teen years, and I found it excruciating to discuss with anybody, even though I was raised in the faith and had plenty of well-meaning adults to talk about it with. I'd grown up religious enough, but I got a little intense about it as I got older. I could pinpoint distinctions between mortal sin and venial sin on episodes of *Welcome Back, Kotter* (Horshack didn't know the vitamins were drugs) or *What's Happening!!* (oh, Rerun, you knew bootlegging that Doobie Brothers show would break Michael McDonald's heart).

I was an altar boy until I was sixteen, which is pretty late to stop, but I didn't fit into the cassock and surplice anymore. I still went to CCD classes after confirmation, which hardly anyone does. Of course, I was the only boy in the CCD class. Once my teacher had asked the girls in the class, "Who's he going with?"

Regina Kelley (who of course reported this entire discussion to my sisters immediately afterward) said, "Well, he's kind of *shy*." The teacher said, "Awww, that's the best kind!" I was mortified when my sisters told me about this—once your CCD teacher is trying to find you a date, your social life is probably a matter for St. Jude, the patron saint of hopeless cases.

For me, religion was an escape from the world, not a connection to it. I gleaned all my religious ideas from books and kept it all fiercely private. I went to confession at four on Saturday afternoons, the only time of the week they had confessions, because nobody went except the same five or six old ladies, who were more weirded out than gratified by my presence. I kept confession note cards in my pocket so I wouldn't forget any of my sins, even though I never really had any juicy dirt to share. I never even rode my bike, for fear somebody I knew would pass by St. Mary's on Saturday afternoon and see my bike in the bicycle rack. The priests of the parish, who were all extremely kind and friendly guys, would usually try to cheer me up. They seemed puzzled but glad to see me, and we'd chat about the Red Sox, who were testing our faith something fierce.

One nice thing about growing up Catholic is it makes you open-minded about other people's religions, since ours is nuttier than yours. I believed lots of nutty things, so many that I'm never surprised at the dumb shit other people believe. I always looked forward to the annual Mass where we'd renew our baptismal vows. ("Do you renounce the glamour of eeeeviiiiil?" Who wrote this script, Ozzy?) Being a pop fan is a lot like Catholic devotion—

lots of ritual, lots of ceremony, lots of private oblations as we genuflect before our sacred spaces. We touch the icon to enter the sacred space, genuflecting to reliquaries and ostentatoria that make something splendid of our most secret desires and agonies.

I always believed rock stars knew more about everything than I did, so I was always relating them to religion. I pondered the existence of God because Billy Idol did. I questioned the connections between sexual freedom and spiritual concentration because Prince sang about them.

My beliefs basically bordered on idolatry. I was like the Israelites in the book of Exodus when they're always getting caught with false idols, because God can't turn his back without his people cheating on him with some Babylonian fish god or golden calf. The whole Bible read like one long episode of *Three's Company*, with the people of God as Jack Tripper, always getting busted in a "two dates for the same night" episode, with God as the jealous cuckold dumping a drink over their heads.

Being a hermit was my vice. Not necessarily a bad vice; it protected me from other, more interesting vices I could have been discovering, which may have left more damage behind. I guess, strictly speaking, it was not even a vice in itself—more like what Catholics of my parents' generation used to call a "habitual disposition," a tendency to have trouble avoiding specific occasions of sin. I was in the market for some snazzier vices, some that would actually teach me something.

Lourdes was nothing like I pictured it. From books, I had imagined a peaceful solemn spot in the woods, a quiet little grotto where I could enjoy an unmediated, unspoiled moment with true divinity. Instead, it was like Las Vegas. There were neon lights everywhere, signs for motels and gift shops, stands selling special Lourdes candles. There were tourists everywhere. And I loved it. I loved how Las Vegas it was, and my main emotion was relief. I loved all the electric glare and all the noise. I loved hearing all the excitement in all the different languages and accents. It wasn't so different from going to a hard-core all-ages show at a punk club on a Saturday afternoon, brushing up against other people's bodies, letting go of my boundaries, trying not to get spooked about the push and rush of the crowd.

I didn't dare to tell my family a thing about what an intense experience I was having. I held on to my candle and listened to the other pilgrims sing. I didn't have any miracles to pray for—I wasn't there looking for a cure or a sign. I just stared and tried to take it all in. I had shown up as a nineteen-year-old tourist who knew everything and suddenly I felt like I didn't have the answer to a damn thing. It was frightening, obviously, but just like a punk rock show, it was also exciting.

I've tried to purge the religion from my system, and I'm always frustrated that I can't. No matter how hard I have tried to pry that Catholic block out from inside my head, the best I can settle for is being a bad Catholic. It's like Lou Reed said to Lester Bangs about drugs: "I've never made any bones about the fact that I take amphetamines. Any sane person would every chance they get. But I'm not in favor of legalization, because I don't want all those idiots running around grinding their teeth at me." That's basically how I feel about religion. It's a drug I abuse, but I don't want to see it on the street.

This relationship is not a romance. God is not a girlfriend—she is a roommate's girlfriend, one you put up with having around. You can break up with your roommate, and you can break up with your girlfriend, but you can't break up with your roommate's girlfriend, and even when you're both through with the roommate, you can't break up with each other. Long after you've moved out and they're broken up, she will still be coming up to you at parties and saying hi. You will run into her at the library where she works or the bar where she pulls pints. You will not make a scene, because (it's a fact) people are more polite to their roommates' girlfriends than they are to their own girlfriends or their own roommates, for that matter. You will not give her the "You remind me of an apartment I wish I could forget I got trapped in" face, or the "I've heard you through the walls screaming the name of that deadbeat who skipped out on the phone bill" face.

You will, instead, feel vaguely sorry for her. She doesn't know anyone else at this party. You are who she's talking to and it's not fair? Why you? Why her? Great, now she's going to need a fucking ride home. She is suffering and she is maybe even bleeding and this is not at all your problem, so why won't she learn to take care of herself for once?

That's still basically my conception of God—a stoner chick who hasn't eaten any solid food all weekend and won't admit it. She makes disastrous decisions and says things she hasn't thought through. When I try to commune with God, I'm basically talking to this stoner chick and trying to suggest politely that she eat something. "Hey, I'm really interested in what you're saying right now, and I can't wait to continue this discussion, so let me make you a sandwich and we can keep going, okay?"

When I was nineteen, I seriously thought that if I solved the problem of religion, I would get out of having to think about all this stupid stuff. It always makes me mad that I never solved it. I did not expect to still be furious about these things when I was an adult—but then, I didn't expect to still be buying a new Madonna album every year either, and since Madonna was so fearless and rosary-flashing on the surface, yet so crucified and mortified on the inside, she probably still gets pissed about religion too. She even named her daughter Lourdes. Since Madonna, like so many other hell-raising teenage girls, has gone on in adulthood to be a bit of a religious bore, I guess she wasn't as bold and independent as I thought she was at the time—she was probably just as fucked up and scared as I was. She must have taught me something about feeling a little pity for the gods. But it's more likely she was feeling pity for me.

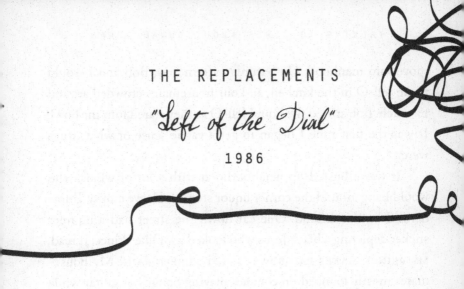

The bus came every afternoon, right on time. Every forty minutes, the New Haven city bus rumbled down Whalley Avenue, and I could see it from my bedroom window. The billboard on the side had Judge Wapner's face and the tag line "Today Is Judgment Day!" I never got on the bus—I just waited to see that billboard as it rolled past my block. Proof that the word never runs out of trivial omens for ominously inclined adolescents, which is another thing the world never runs out of. Omens like this were a dime a dozen, and I was the sucker with the pocketful of dimes.

I was living with a houseful of hippies in New Haven, sleeping on a futon in the corner of my friend Bob's room. It was the first time I was living on my own, paying rent. It felt like a bold move into manhood. On Saturday afternoons, Bob and I would make Jell-O in the kitchen, and our housemates crowded around to watch. Bob stirred the liquid Jell-O as they stared into the bowl. It was the first time I began to get a vague sense of what drugs were.

It was a busted-up neighborhood with a lot of winos, who would hang around the corner liquor store and leave empty Thunderbird bottles around. One car down the street had a bumper sticker depicting a black Jesus who looked a lot like Prince. It read, MY PRINCE MAKES RAINBOWS . . . NOT PURPLE RAIN! My housemates mostly lounged on couches playing bongos or guitar while I made us all peanut butter sandwiches and wrote tortured love letters to a red-haired girl in Nova Scotia.

I had a job at the library shelving books, living on my daily bread of two Wawa dogs with extra cheese and a thirty-two-ounce Coke ($1.69). Every day around noon, I woke up, rolled over and pressed play on the boom box by my futon, drowsily contemplating the day ahead of me as the Replacements blasted out of the speakers. Before work, I would laze away the afternoon under a tree, reading St. Augustine's *Confessions*. That spring, I had read *Ulysses* and *Portrait of the Artist* for the first time, and they had really shaken up my Irish Catholic applecart. I was full of questions about God and the universe. The answers, obviously, were all there in my boom box.

The Replacements made me feel a little less scared, because they made good imaginary friends. They looked like a band that would actually be fun to be in. Some bands just lend themselves to that fantasy, like Lynyrd Skynyrd or Earth, Wind & Fire—they looked like you could just drop in and they wouldn't even notice you were hanging around for at least two albums. Jonathan Richman once said he formed a band because he was lonely. The Replacements were imaginary friends who I could practice on while I was learning to have actual friends.

At night, everybody would gather on the couch to watch TV with the sound down, through a haze of bong smog, flipping channels while listening to Laurie Anderson. The goal was to find cosmic random synchronicities in the airwaves of the collective unconscious. One night, they flipped to a Superman cartoon during "O Superman." Everybody freaked and ran out of the room. There was another hippie house on our block with some guys who called their band Acidemix. The only song they knew was "Bela Lugosi's Dead," but they could play it for hours.

The neighborhood kids hung out in our yard, mainly because of Nick, who had a boa constrictor in his room. Once Nick let the kids come up to see Bo, we had the most popular house on the block. They lined up every evening for Bo's dinner. Nick would bike home from Woolworth's with a mouse in a cardboard box. The front of the box read, I'VE FOUND A HOME! The other side of the box read, SOMEBODY REALLY LOVES ME! The cover photo showed a boy and girl happily frolicking with their new hamster.

"Is he gonna eat that thing?"

"Damn."

"Is he gonna kill it first?"

"Is the mouse dead?"

"I can see him."

"He's got to be dead now."

After the snake had chowed down on the mouse, and the kids had finished screaming, Nick tossed the empty box out into the hallway, where they piled up and formed a little memorial pyramid. Every night, I came home from work and tiptoed to my room, stepping over the pile of I'VE FOUND A HOME! boxes.

I did a lot of things for the first time that summer: signed a lease, drank beer, drank coffee, gave myself a haircut, smoked pot, smoked Play-Doh (it took us all evening to realize it wasn't really hash). I learned to wash dishes and make pasta. I drew the line at sex and hacky sack. One roommate, Matt, lost his virginity while I slept through the whole thing. Jorge Luis Borges died the night I smoked pot for the first time. There I was the morning after, groggily sitting in the backyard, lost in the circular ruins of Catholic guilt, and I read in the paper that one of my all-time literary idols had died overnight and I felt certain that God was punishing the whole world for my transgression.

Everybody in the house played music. We'd sit out on the porch all night, with Jeffrey and James on guitar, Nick on bongos and David on flute. Jeffrey and I wrote poetic ballads of torment and squalor (sample title: "My Baby's Sleeping in a Burning House"). Jeffrey tried to teach me guitar, since I was desperate to join their jam sessions, but my fingers would not obey the merciless lashings of my muse. My burning desire to be the new Bob Dylan was severely hampered by the fact that I couldn't even master the fucking chords to "Love Stinks."

Occasionally they took off to follow the Dead's summer tour, after Jerry got out of his coma. I went to the Dylan show at Madison Square Garden, a massive pilgrimage for me. His backing band was Tom Petty and the Heartbreakers, who didn't seem to know any of his songs, so every song sounded exactly like Billy Idol's "White Wedding." But what the hell—I got to see Dylan. We also decided to make a pilgrimage to every spot in New York that was mentioned in a Lou Reed song. We started out at Union Square but chickened out on the walk up to Lexington 1-2-5.

I also went to see the Replacements in Providence. It was the best night of my life up to that point, no question. It was an all-ages show at the Living Room. The opener was a local hard-core band called That'll Learn Ya. Paul Westerberg and Bob Stinson were out on the floor, watching the band. That was the first time I'd ever seen the guys in the headlining band come out to stand in the crowd with the rest of us. They didn't blend in, though. Paul Westerberg had these big, stripey, '70s dork pants on. Bob Stinson was wearing a toga.

While Westerberg was sitting over at the bar, my roommate nudged me and we went over to say hi. I froze up and couldn't utter a word, but he smiled and shook our hands, then said, "Well, gents, I'm gonna finish my Kool." When he headed backstage, I eyeballed the butt in the ashtray. I only hesitated a second before I pounced. I carried that crushed Kool filter in my pocket all night like an amulet.

I had a wad of cotton I'd saved from aspirin bottles. Up front by the stage, I stuffed some cotton in my ears and passed it to the girl next to me, who took some and passed it on. She smiled. I smiled back. The Replacements came on and started with "Hold My Life." It was pure noise, pure destruction. Everybody was pushing and thrashing and jumping—I was too. Paul Westerberg howled through his hair about small-town losers and big-town vices. Tommy Stinson sucked in his cheeks and preened for the ladies. Bob Stinson kept telling us, "Ya gotta boo!" The dude next to me kept throwing elbows and screaming for "Take Me Down to the Hospital."

The Replacements jumped from one song to another—"Left of the Dial," "I Will Dare," "Bastards of Young." They did the first verse of "Kiss Me on the Bus," then got bored and trailed off. Paul said, "Okay, you sissies, this is an Aerosmith song," and ripped into "My Fist Your Face." They did the *Green Acres* theme, with Paul as Eddie Albert and Tommy as Eva Gabor. They started fucking around and switching instruments, with Paul playing drums for "Waitress in the Sky." They lurched offstage, leaving Bob alone to do a solo version of "What Is and What Should Never Be." When none of them were left standing, the Young Fresh Fellows came onstage, took their instruments and finished the show. "We're the replacements for the Replacements," the singer announced. They sucked. It was awesome.

I couldn't even describe what a great night that was. I felt indestructible, or at least undestroyed, more alive than I'd ever been. I walked out of the show feeling like I could do anything, dare anything, just jump into anything. Us against the world. I was used to feeling "me against the world," but "us against the world" was a lot more fun. My ears rang all the way home and I didn't want them to stop. It made me want to go start something. It was the greatest punk rock show I had ever seen.

I still had the Kool butt I stole from Paul Westerberg's ashtray. I took it home. The next day I mailed it to the girl in Nova Scotia. She wrote back, "It stinks to high heaven." Clearly, she and I were not meant to be. But the Replacements and I? Meant to be. *So* meant to be.

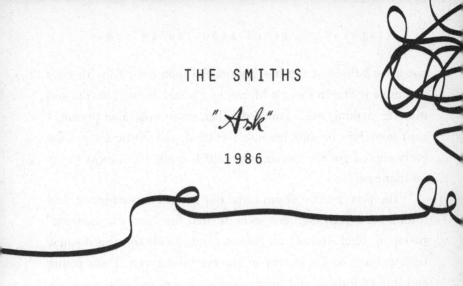

THE SMITHS

"Ask"

1986

You know the scene at the end of *St. Elmo's Fire* where everybody's saying good-bye to Rob Lowe at the bus station? Rob Lowe takes Judd Nelson's arm, looks him in the eye and whispers, "Don't let her go." Judd hangs his head, because he knows that Rob Lowe is right (as he always is) and that he needs to hold on tight to Ally Sheedy, even if she did just bang Andrew McCarthy in the shower. That's a beautiful moment.

Well, right now, think of me as Rob Lowe, urging you to cling to Ally Sheedy, or whatever she may happen to symbolize in your own life. (For me, Ally Sheedy represents the Taoist concept of "Wind over Fire," but I'm not going to lay that on you now.)

We all have our Ally Sheedys, the things we cling to and do

not leave behind at the bus station. All men have Ally Sheedys and mine is Steven Patrick Morrissey. He has devoted his life and mine to making me a lamer, dumber, more miserable person. I can't leave him behind, because I've tried, and yet he follows me everywhere I go. Six years on my trail? I should be so lucky to get off that easy.

The first Smiths album came out when I was eighteen, and it took me exactly eighteen seconds (that first "and you maaaade" swoop in "Reel Around the Fountain") to decide this was my new favorite band in the history of the everythingverse. I was young and impressionable and hungry for guidance, and this guy knew everything.

Morrissey was my Mrs. Garrett, the house mother from *The Facts of Life*, a soothing adult figure giving me words of wisdom.

"Aw, Steven Patrick . . . I'm a little depressed."

"There'll be blood on the cleaver tonight."

"Excuse me?"

"You should never go to them. Let them come to you. Just like I do."

"Wow! I never saw it that way, but you're right!"

"I decree today that life is simply taking and not giving. England is mine and it owes me a living."

"Gosh, me too, Steven Patrick! But I have a problem. See, there's this girl I like."

"She wants it now and she will not wait. But she's too rough and I'm too delicate."

"I wish I could talk to her, but I don't know how."

"Pretty girls make graves."

"They do? That's terrible!"

"If I were you, I wouldn't bother."

"Thanks, Steven Patrick! You're the *best*!"

I cannot even begin to calculate how much truly terrible advice I got from Morrissey. In the endless *Tuesdays with Morrissey* conversations I had with him, in the privacy of my own overheated skull, he gave me a map to life, with all the arrows pointing in contrary directions. If he was Mrs. Garrett, I was happy to be his Blair, Tootie, Natalie and Jo combined.

"Nobody understands me, Steven Patrick. Nobody but you!"

"People said you were easily led, and they were half right."

"Wow! Will I ever make friends?"

"Does the body rule the mind, or does the mind rule the body?"

"Excuse me?"

"I dunno."

"Oh. Me neither, Steven Patrick! But what about that girl?"

"Love is just a miserable lie."

"I love you, Steven Patrick! You know *so much* about these things!"

His songs were a Magic 8-Ball of the damned. Whenever I would contemplate a really big adventure, like maybe washing my hair and putting on clean socks and leaving my room, Morrissey was there to talk me out of it and provide me with excellent reasons to keep hiding in my room where I belonged. When I did go out, to attend class or pick up a bag of Zeus Chips, I felt guilty for cheating on Morrissey with life.

He was perfect at expressing the fascistic demands on life that sensitive boys routinely make on the planet. I agreed completely. The failure of the rest of the world to arrange itself according to my moods, whims and desire to be recognized as a genius without actually doing anything—why, that was just proof that this was the wrong planet to be born on, and Morrissey knew I deserved better. Who were all these people I had to deal with every day? Why did I give them my valuable time? Girls, man. You try to talk to them, they just tell you things like "You've been in the house too long."

Whenever I played him for other people, they usually winced and said, "Jesus, that man cannot sing." This was proof of my sensitive ear, and proof that Morrissey and I only really understood each other. My mom thought he was cute, but that's about it, although she really just liked his last name. "Morrissey!" she said. "He could be a Kerry boy!"

I was just going through the basic paradox of adolescence, which Mozz was remarkably candid about: I Want the One I Can't Have, and It's Driving Me Mad. One hundred percent of teenagers dream about making out, but they only dream about making out with 5 percent of other teenagers. This means our dreams and our realities are barely on speaking terms, so we look forward to making out with people who aren't real, keeping us in a nearly universal state of teen frustration. It screws us up for the rest of our lives, as we keep hoping for the unattainable. It's like if you planned your whole life around meeting Garfield, the cartoon cat. I do not know anyone who claims they want to own a cat someday, but they're holding out for Garfield. If I met somebody who broke up with their cats every few weeks and said, "He just doesn't eat lasagna" or "I don't know, he was nice, but seldom seemed to be thinking sassy wisecracks about the slobbering dog," I would have to assume this person was an idiot. Yet practically every teenager on earth channels their deepest sexual and romantic yearnings into fantasies.

Why are we designed this way? Who knows? I was in the flush of young manhood, with all the supposed vigor of youth, yet I was surly and hostile to everyone I met, including myself. I let my Walkman do the talking, and all it had to say was "Stay away." I would have been this way even if I'd never heard the Smiths—but it was Morrissey who convinced me my most appalling qualities were heroic achievements. I guess that's what rock stars are for.

I took being a Smiths fan seriously. I wondered what "vicars" or "moors" or "rusty spanners" were. I was mesmerized by the way Morrissey pronounced words such as "plagiarize," "guts" and "delicate"—was that a Brit thing, or just him? I loved the song where Morrissey confessed he had a nightmare that lasted 20 years, 7 months, and 27 days. Assuming he meant his life, I calculated that I would turn this precise age on September 29, and eagerly awaited the revelations that would greet me. As it turned out, nothing happened that day at all, although I recall eating some frozen waffles.

I imagined myself as intimately familiar with the geography of Manchester, just from hearing Morrissey sing about it. The guy was sure into locations—under the iron bridge, the alley by the railway station, the fountain, the patio, the scholarly room, the darkened underpass, the YWCA—whew. That's a lot of turf to cover, especially for a guy who never moved out of his mom's house. Yet as Morrissey understood, my room was the scariest place of all.

I broke up with Morrissey after the second Smiths album, *Meat Is Murder*, came out in the spring of 1985, because he was just . . . too much of a jerk. I was desperate to get out of the hum-drum town Morrissey had helped me build in my brain. My life had gotten totally grim—I just sat around my dorm room in a depressive stupor, too distracted by gloom to get any work done, too afraid to shave or answer the phone or go outside. Morrissey had turned into a lame self-parody, and so had I.

I have to admit, it was acrimonious. I went from idolizing the Smiths to despising them. Shit got ugly. I blamed them for all my problems—and if that didn't make me a true Smiths fan, what could? Hell, Morrissey had taught me everything I knew about blaming my bad personality on people I'd never met. In a way, hating him was my sincerest possible act of fandom. Like Darth Vader light-sabering Obi-Wan Kenobi, I proved the douchebag student had become the douchebag master.

But I taped over *Meat Is Murder* with the new Madonna album, *Like a Virgin*. She was another pushy, needy egomaniac as untrustworthy as Morrissey, equally full of bullshit and bent on my destruction, but I had a feeling it was time to pay her brand of bullshit more attention. At least she had something to teach me that I didn't already know. And even though I was disturbed by her worldview, I liked her songs a lot better than "Meat Is Murder."

I started forcing myself to leave my room, going to indie rock shows, even when I didn't feel like it. The club DJs would put on Smiths records, and the big-hair new-wave girls would perk up whenever their songs came on. What was wrong with these girls?

Then, just when I'd gone to all the trouble of purging the Smiths out of my system, they did something really offensive, which is they got good again. The first night my friend Martha played me *The Queen Is Dead* in her room, I was consumed with rage at the fact that it was so unmistakably, ridiculously great, and the fact that Morrissey was making fun of himself and doing a much better job of it than I could. Morrissey had beaten me to making all the changes I wanted to make—he was now funny, self-deprecating, apologetic about what an asshole he'd been to me, and (unfor-fucking-givable) blatantly trying to make me like him again. Bastard. I hated him more than ever, and decided to never listen to the Smiths again.

I was up in Boston for the weekend, kicking around the record shops on a cool summer evening. I ran into a guy I hadn't seen since high school. Vincent had changed a lot. He was now bleaching his hair. He was out of the closet. He was obviously hitting the gym. And he was obviously a Smiths fan. It must sound pretty weird, but this was a time when the only people in the world who dressed like Morrissey were Morrissey fans, so we could spot one another pretty easily.

I was wearing a cardigan, and Vincent was wearing a lime green tank top, so it only took a minute for us to start chatting about the Smiths. We found somewhere to sit and eat french fries. The Red Sox game was on TV. We talked barely at all about high school, a great deal about gender ambiguity in "Still Ill," and a little about the Red Sox. He wasn't a baseball fan, so he was curious about what was happening on the field.

"This guy is Wade Boggs."

"He looks like a charming man."

"He is. He's a singles-hitting third baseman who never knew his place."

"Who's that?"

"Dwight Evans, right field."

"He is his mother's only son, and he's a desperate one."

It was rare to spend a whole night talking about music with somebody I vaguely knew. He knew all these details about Morrissey I didn't know—the way he revered James Dean, the name of the French actor on the cover of *The Queen Is Dead*. We debated whether Keats and Yeats versus Wilde was really a fair fight, given that Wilde idolized Keats and once kissed the soil on his grave in Rome.

"What the hell was that?"

"A double play," I explained. "The runner on third got caught."

"Will he get home?"

"He hasn't got one."

"Barbarism begins at home."

We didn't have many friends in common, so we ran out of gossip fast, but we just kept talking in our private Smiths language. By the end of the game, we'd discussed *The Queen Is Dead* to death, and I'd learned which members of the 1986 Red Sox were hot. Jim Rice grounded into a 6–4–3.

"That's it?" Vincent asked. "It's over."

"It's over."

"In a way, it never really began."

"But in my heart, it was so real."

We shook hands at the train and traded addresses. We never wrote those letters and never ran into each other again. I thought it was strange to spend an evening having so much fun with someone I didn't know so well, and to not hang out after that, because I was too young to know adult life is full of accidents and interrupted moments and empty beds you climb into and don't climb out of. A few months later, the Red Sox lost the World Series.

One night that winter, I went to an indie rock show at the Grotto and the DJ played the new Smiths import twelve-inch "Ask." I couldn't believe Morrissey was admitting he was wrong about all that stuff he'd said a couple years earlier. He was coming right out and saying that people being nice to one another was a good thing, not a sign of weakness or moral corruption. I was stunned to hear it, partly because it was my old nemesis Morrissey saying it but partly because I was hoping it was a lie. It sounded like so much work, I didn't know if I could handle it. But he made it sound like trying would be fun.

I was leaning against a wall in the Grotto, watching the usual big-hair new-wave girls do their usual "oooh, we love the Smiths!" dance, and completely failing to muster up any of the bile against them that had once made me feel so safe and strong and adult. I was just a kid leaning against a wall in a smelly rock club, enjoying some mediocre guitar bands, and avoiding eye contact with anyone. I had big problems, and Morrissey wanted me to know that, but he also wanted me to know that they were temporary problems. He and I had been through a lot together, but nothing would ever come between us again. And alas, nothing ever did. I haven't been able to get rid of this guy since.

Some things annoy you forever, and some disappear. It's impossible to predict. For instance, throughout the 1980s and well into the 1990s, people made little quote marks with their fingers when they said something "clever" or "ironic." God, that was annoying. I assumed it was going to bug the shit out of me forever. And then, for some reason, people stopped. If you're under thirty, you have never made little quote marks with your fingers. When you watch *Say Anything*, you think it just looks silly when that girl tells Ione Skye, "I know we used to be [quote fingers] 'ultra competitive.'" You probably wonder what's wrong with her.

I don't know how this massive cultural change happened so

suddenly, with no public outcry or debate—but it did. America, we got this one right. How did this [quote fingers] "happen"?

The same thing with the way people on an airplane used to clap when the plane landed. I guess if the plane crashed, we were supposed to just fold our arms and boo? I assumed, without giving it much thought, this was going to annoy me for the rest of my life (along with everything else about air travel). Then sometime in the late 1990s, I noticed that air applause had died out. Nobody talked about not clapping anymore—they just stopped clapping.

Some annoyances persist forever, like the Eagles or "last time I checked." Some are gone before you know it, like Dire Straits or Paris Hilton. You can't tell which is which until it's too late. I mean, everybody assumed Wilson Phillips were going to stick around for years. If I'd known how temporary they were, I would have enjoyed them more.

But there's one prediction I feel confident in making. "No worries" is going to annoy people forever.

"No worries" is the best thing to happen to sullen teenagers since I was one—even better than vampire sexting, GTL or Call of Duty: Modern Warfare 2. When I was a sullen teenager, we had to make do with the vastly inferior "whatever."

"No worries" beats "whatever" six ways to Sunday. It's a vaguely mystical way of saying "I hear your mouth make noise, saying something that I plan to ignore." It has a noble Rasta-man vibe, as if you're quoting some sort of timeless yet meaningless proverb on the nature of change—"Soon come," or "As the cloud is slow, the wind is quick." In terms of ignoring provocation, "no worries" is just about perfect.

I first noticed it at a rock show in the late '90s, where somebody was accidentally kicking my friend's calves. When this was pointed out to him, he smiled and said, "No worries!" Three times in a row. But the fourth time, he finally understood what we were saying and stopped kicking. He was a perfectly friendly and agreeable guy. He just hadn't even *heard* us, because he had a magic shield to protect him. He had "no worries." I did a *Rolling Stone* article on MTV's Carson Daly, which meant following him around all day while people bugged him for decisions or reactions or favors. He kept saying, "Yeah, no worries," which struck me as the most brilliant possible response to any stupid request. Suddenly, "whatever" was just not sullen enough.

Every time you say "no worries," you have chosen a nonaggressive and nonconfrontational way to inform me it's not your problem, and I admire you for that. It's a bit like "ma'am," an expression I picked up living in the South and wondered how I'd ever functioned without it. You can say "ma'am" to mean anything from "Excuse me, you're blocking this supermarket aisle" to "I'm sure the flight attendant would put that in the storage bin for you" to "Are you really pretending not to notice the line starts over here?" But "ma'am" doesn't translate in the North, where it just startles and offends. In my hometown, "ma'am" is something only a hit man would say. The first time I tried it was when I was driving around in Randolph with my dad, looking for the bakery where we were supposed to pick up my sister's wedding cake.

He pulled over and said, "Ask this lady for directions." I rolled down my window, cleared my throat for the nice Irish woman in her front yard weeding the hedges and said, "Ma'aaaaam?" She jumped about a foot in the air.

When we pulled away, my dad asked, "Why did you call her man?"

"I didn't. I called her 'ma'am.'"

"You what?"

There was no defense.

What I should have said was, "No worries, Dad." But sadly, this hadn't been invented yet.

When John Hughes died in the summer of 2009, I grieved because he'd never gotten to use "no worries" in a movie, though he'd already given us so much. Being a sullen teenager when those John Hughes movies came out—well, it must have been like how it felt to be a real-life button man in the Gambino family when Al Pacino started making gangster flicks. Today we remember those films as a unit, but they came out one by one, year by year. After seeing one installment, we had to wait months for the next. We had no way of knowing *Sixteen Candles* was a bridge to the still-unimaginable *Breakfast Club*. And we had no way of knowing they would culminate in *Pretty in Pink*, the apex of the Molly Trilogy. Hughes personally had nothing to do with *St. Elmo's Fire*, but since it came out between *The Breakfast Club* and *Pretty in Pink*, it went into the canon too—it was to the Molly Trilogy what *Mean Streets* is to the *Godfather* movies.

Throw in *Weird Science*, *Ferris Bueller's Day Off* and *Some Kind of Wonderful* and you get the mythic canon of an ur-American teen utopia. Thanks to years of weekend-afternoon reruns, these movies still define high school agony, even for kids (especially girls) who weren't born when they came out. You're never more than a few minutes away from hearing somebody quote Anthony Michael Hall ("Could you describe the ruckus, sir?") or Judd Nelson ("All I need is a lobotomy and some tights"). This guy could really describe a ruckus. He knew how to listen.

When he died, it was startling to realize how famous he was, especially since he hadn't directed a movie in years. But despite his reclusive ways, he was arguably Hollywood's most famous director. Even at the time, he was as famous as the Brat Packers in his movies—when *Pretty in Pink* came out, everyone called it the new "John Hughes movie," even though he'd farmed out the actual directing to his associate Howard Deutch. In the 2001 sleaze comedy *Not Another Teen Movie* (one of my favorite films of the past decade, to my shame), the kids go to John Hughes High, while the football team plays in Harry Dean Stadium.

It's a sign of how 1980s teen culture keeps on resonating—even people who were born in the '90s can O.D. on borrowed nostalgia for the unremembered '80s. Maybe that's because it was an era when teen trash was the only corner of pop culture that wasn't a high-gloss fraud. Movies for adults sucked in the 1980s, and music for adults sucked even worse; whether we're talking Kathleen Turner flicks or Steve Winwood albums, the decade's non-teen culture has no staying power at all. The only sign of life *was* teen trash, the most despised, frivolous and temporary stuff out there. Alyssa Milano wasn't lying: "Teen steam! You gotta let it out!"

To simplify brutally, there were really only two kinds of movies in the '80s:

(1) Movies in which Judd Nelson might conceivably pump his fist while crossing the football field

(2) Movies in which Mickey Rourke sweats a lot and symbolizes something

It goes without saying that the first kind remains lingua franca, while the second kind was forgotten by the time the '90s started and seems both hideously dated and joyless now. One of the reasons we remember these movies so clearly is that they were so much more honest than the Hollywood adult movies of the day. There was a feeling of expensive mendacity to all the aging baby-boomer dramas, all those sensitive flicks with William Hurt or Michael Douglas or Melanie Griffith backlit with baby oil all over the lens. The moment that sums it up for me is the truly loathsome opening shot of *Top Gun*, with the caption "Indian Ocean: Present Day." That totally sums up where Hollywood culture was at in 1986: the ruling principle was that the "Present Day" would always look, sound and feel exactly like 1986—too horrible a thought to even contemplate.

There was already a glorious teen movie boom before John Hughes showed up. In 1982 we got *Fast Times at Ridgemont High*, which still gets my vote as the decade's best movie. But in the early '80s we also got *Class*, *Risky Business*, *Getting It On*, *The Last American Virgin*, *Private School*, *Paradise*, *The Legend of Billie Jean*, *The Beach Girls*, *Vision Quest*, *Footloose*, *Flashdance* and many more. *Girls Just Want to Have Fun* is one of the all-time best movies about growing up Catholic, with Sarah Jessica Parker as the bespectacled geek girl who longs to go on *Dance-TV*, and Helen Hunt as her wisecracking friend ("Hail Mary? Sorry Sister, I thought you meant 'Proud Mary,' but I do a great Tina Turner!"). Even the nuns in this movie get to be cool. *Dirty Dancing* was just a big-budget copy of this movie, although an admittedly great one. (Hard to go wrong with Patrick Swayze.) People obsess about the strangest teen movies. When I'm walking around in Greenpoint, my neighborhood in Brooklyn, I always take a loop around McGolrick Park to the side street where one of my neighbors is parked with a license plate that reads WORDMAN. I always think, damn, that is one hard-core *Eddie and the Cruisers* fan. And who thought that in 2010, there'd be any kind of *Eddie and the Cruisers* fan?

The teen movie explosion was mostly garbage, sure. But as a rebellion against smug Hollywood pap, the garbage meant something. And Phoebe Cates? She *really* meant something.

John Hughes's movies were special because they had the sassiest girls, the cattiest boys, the most relatable boy-girl friendships and bumbling parents and big sisters on muscle relaxants. For those of us who were sullen teenagers, it shocked us how he got the details right, especially the music. "I'd rather be making music than movies," he said in 1985, describing himself as a frustrated guitarist. "*Pretty in Pink* was written to the Psychedelic Furs, Lou Reed and Mott the Hoople. *The Breakfast Club* was written in my Clash–Elvis Costello period."

That's how we got the *Pretty in Pink* soundtrack, one of the defining '80s new-wave albums. You could complain that when the Psychedelic Furs did their remake of "Pretty in Pink" for this movie, it was about one-third as good as the original. I would counter that until this movie, girls never listened to the original; once "Pretty in Pink" became a song girls actually liked, it became a totally different song.

His movies had loads of talk; it's no coincidence that the generation weaned on *The Breakfast Club* was the generation that decided John Cassavetes was the great American filmmaker. I first fell for Molly Ringwald in a movie where she plays John Cassavetes' daughter, Miranda to his Prospero, in the 1982 Shakespeare update *Tempest*. When a cute American boy arrives to rescue her from desert island drudgery, the first thing she asks him is "So is punk still big in the States?"

But John Hughes didn't bother trying to catch how teens "really" talked, which then as now just meant "um" and "you know." Instead, he indulged his genius for invented catchphrases. It's not like any of us actually said things like "So I smell" or "While we're on the topic of the double-breasted party machine," but he had an ear for what we were trying to say.

Here's just one example: it's easy to forget now, but *Sixteen Candles* invented the word "geek" as we know it. Before Anthony Michael Hall played the kid listed in the credits only as "the

Geek," geeks were just called "wusses" or other homophobic epithets. The word "geek" was just an arcane reference to the old Dr. Demento novelty "Pencil Neck Geek." (It doesn't come up once in *Fast Times*, which goes for "wuss" instead.) The geek as a social category didn't exist before *Sixteen Candles* entered the Anthony Michael Hall of Fame. Now, can you imagine a day without that word? Hughes knew geekdom: he even did a cameo as Hall's dad in *The Breakfast Club*, picking him up with an E MC2 license plate. (This joke helped the geeks in the theater figure out where all the other geeks were sitting, since we were the ones who laughed.)

To me, his most famous and beloved creation is Duckie, from *Pretty in Pink*. It has been suggested in some quarters that Duckie is, in fact, the Messiah. This suggestion is probably correct. The parallels are daunting: Jon Cryer and Jesus Christ? Practically the same name! Both are poor Jewish boys with absent fathers. Both make the ultimate sacrifice so that others may have life—or, if they prefer, Andrew McCarthy. Duckie tells Andie, "I would have died for you!" Both have a very special relationship with Dweezil Zappa. Duck of God, you take away the sins of the world; grant us peace.

The Duckman is at the heart of the central question of the John Hughes universe: Why, Andie, why? Why does Molly's character go for hot richie Blaine (McCarthy) when she could have the lavishly moussed Duckie? It's amazing how violently people argue over the end of *Pretty in Pink*. To this day, there's a popular legend that the original version of the movie had Andie choosing Duckie, except it supposedly got changed after test screenings.

I'll believe this when I see it—but given that this scene has never shown up anywhere, not even in the DVD outtakes, I'm going to keep believing this "lost original" is a myth that just illustrates how much people love Duckie.

I love Duckie too, but what makes him Duckie is the selfless way he accepts the ruckus of female desire, and the way he wants her to get what she wants. So he urges Andie to go dance with Blaine, even though Blaine's a jerk, and even though Blaine showed up to the prom wearing an even goofier outfit than Duckie's. And of course, Duckie ends up getting jumped by another girl—Kristy Swanson!—before the song even ends. That's teen utopia for you.

Those final seconds of *Pretty in Pink* will always be controversial—but they sum up why I will always love John Hughes movies. The sullen teenager inside me needs Duckie to set Molly free, and so the sullen teenager inside me will go to his grave defending that final scene. *Pretty in Pink* shows why sullen teenagers will always exist and will always annoy people. You disagree? Hey—no worries.

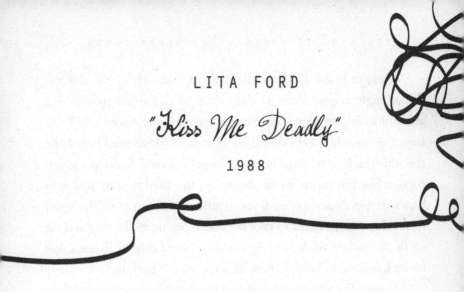

LITA FORD

"Kiss Me Deadly"

1988

Let's spend a few minutes on this girl, which in all honesty is more than she spent on me.

Paula was a messed-up Catholic girl I knew. I liked messed-up Catholic girls. Like a good Catholic boy, I was attracted to messes and to messed-up-ness in general. She was a bartender with long greasy black hair and a denim jacket she wore every day, no matter how hot it was. When I think of the summer of 1988, I think of her. Def Leppard was her band. "Pour Some Sugar on Me" was her tune. Screamin' Joe Elliott? Her man. When Joe howled, "You got the peaches, I got the cream," his voice seemed to herald the imminent union of our peaches, our cream and other sundries from the produce-and-dairy aisle of our hearts.

I got to know Paula at the radio station, where she did the Friday night reggae show. I would drop by to file her records and attempt to impress her. Sometimes she wouldn't show up, and I was forced to cover for her by doing a reggae show, which was kind of like the time the Red Sox had to use George "Boomer" Scott as a pinch runner. She got rowdy when she drank; she liked to start scenes in bars with big dudes and leave me to talk my way out of it. She loved fireworks, and she loved to take her boom box up to the roof and set off bottle rockets while blasting Lita Ford and Guns N' Roses. I was invited, as long as I didn't blow off a thumb or anything.

I spent the summer sleeping alone with a big picture of Morrissey over my bed, ripped out from *Spin* magazine, with an ad for his solo album: "MORRISSEY ... ALONE." Every time I crawled into this bed, I was alone, and for some reason I thought that was a surprising coincidence. Paula hated Morrissey, hated the Cure, hated anything that sounded dour or angsty. But there was always something kind of sad about her. She never liked to talk about her hometown or her history. She had a big, croaky laugh, and her eyes were like clear glass. I could tell she'd come a long way from wherever she was from.

In the afternoons, she called me and we watched *Dial MTV* together over the phone. She kept up a constant motormouth commentary as Adam Curry counted down the top ten viewer requests from 1-900-DIAL-MTV. We sang along with the hits of the summer—"Kiss Me Deadly" and "I Hate Myself for Loving You" and "Sweet Child o' Mine" and "Push It" and "Foolish Beat." Every day, "Pour Some Sugar on Me" was number one.

On weekends we'd sit on her floor listening to records, drinking Jägermeister and Connecticut Cola. All over her wall, she had pictures of Johnny Depp, usually torn out from *Bop* or some other teen fan mag. The show *21 Jump Street* was brand-new that summer. It's hard to remember there even was a time before Johnny Depp was around to toast the loins of our nation . . . but there was. And it was a cold, cold place. She loved to talk about how Johnny Depp was going to change the world. He was a new ideal of manhood, the dawn of a new golden era. It sounded plausible the way she described it. Anything would have.

Paula also had a sweet tooth for pop—Debbie Gibson, Tiffany, Exposé, George Michael—and metal, especially of the ass-kicking girl variety like Lita Ford and Joan Jett. I would come over, bringing her the latest *Bop* magazine, and we'd listen to her Debbie Gibson twelve-inch single of "Only in My Dreams," all the remixes in a row. I would play her my "Foolish Beat" cassingle, with the "Mega Mix" medley of all Debbie's hits. But Paula had big issues with Debbie's video for "Foolish Beat," because she didn't like the boy in the video—too much of a pretty boy. She said, "Debbie should get some bikers in her video."

One night, I helped her make a sign for a political rally she was going to in New York, demonstrating against the nuclear arms race. She made a sign that said, JOHNNY DEPP DEMANDS WORLD PEACE. I stayed up late helping her cut out pictures of Johnny's eyebrows to decorate her sign. She invited me to crash on her floor. We didn't make out or anything, but spending the night in a girl's room was a very big deal. I lay there in the darkness, hearing her breathe. Johnny Depp's eyebrows watched over us both. I remember thinking, "I'm going to remember this night for the rest of my life." What's stranger: the fact that I remember, or the fact that I had a rest of my life? Was there a connection between one fact and the other?

She had to get up early in the morning, because her ride to the rally was coming at six. The clock radio woke us up to Bob Dylan's "Silvio," and we were both too groggy to talk. She got picked up by a married couple in a Volvo; the husband told her to put out her cigarette because "Nobody has ever smoked in this car," which for some reason made us giggle. I staggered home to sleep it off, but I was afraid I would wonder later if it had been a dream, so I wrote a note on an index card and thumbtacked it to the wall: 7 A.M. SHE LIKES ME.

I decided I would make a move, sometime that summer, but it seemed like there was plenty of summer left. My roommates and I threw a house party that turned out kind of like the party Lita Ford sang about in "Kiss Me Deadly," with a truly rancid orange punch my roommate and I had brewed by pouring all the alcohol in the house into a bowl and adding Tang. While people danced in the living room, Paula sat in the kitchen and watched MTV— it was a Rock Block Weekend, so we waited for a Def Leppard block. It didn't take very long. Paula marveled to the "Rock of Ages" video, as Joe Elliott walked into the wizard's castle, pulled the sword from the stone, and lifted it to the heavens. "Excalibur!" she proclaimed.

I figured this was my sign to make a move. So when I walked

her home, I told her I had a crush on her. She said, "Oh, that's nice," but not in a sarcastic way. Her voice sounded sad. She invited me in and turned on MTV. It was a Cher Rock Block. We both sat quaking on her couch. Cher was wearing a black leather jumpsuit and draping herself around her hot young Italian-stallion boyfriend, belting "I Found Someone." Neither of us said a word. What do I do now? Do I say something? Do I lean in to kiss her? Should I say good night?

The next Cher video was the one called "We All Sleep Alone." I said good night.

The next day, Paula called and invited me to a motorcycle festival. Neither of us mentioned the night before. That was a great Cher video.

The highlight of our summer was the night we went to see Debbie Gibson live at the New Haven Coliseum. Naturally, we made Debbie Gibson a mix tape. We loaded it up with punk rock women—the Slits, the Raincoats, X-Ray Spex, Patti Smith. We figured we would toss the tape onstage so Debbie would hear it later and go punk rock. We had the plan down perfect—we even slid the tape into a gift bag that had a teddy bear, since we knew from reading *Bop* that Debbie kept a collection of stuffed animals from her fans. We even wrote our phone numbers on the tape in case Debbie had any questions.

Debbie Gibson was great that night, doing all her hits and a few costume changes. She also did a terrible ballad, "Lost in Your Eyes," as a sign of her mature new direction. What is it with disco girls? Why do they always want to grow up to turn into Barbra

Streisand instead? Paula and I were up front on the floor, sur-rounded by screaming little girls, and we decided Johnny Depp was there in spirit. I sneaked up to throw Debbie our gift bag, but the security guards had other ideas. In fact, they got extremely agitated at the sight of an adult male approaching the stage, which was definitely understandable. I tried to explain I had a present for Debbie, but Tiny and Bruno were not so interested in my mix tape for Debbie, and I was lucky to get back to my seat with all of my teeth.

After the show, we were in the crowd heading out of the Coliseum, and Paula elbowed me. "That's the guy."

"What guy?"

"The video guy."

"Holy shit."

There he was—Debbie's video guy, the guy who played her love interest in the "Foolish Beat" video. There was no mistaking him, with his blue eyes and lofty cheekbones. He was leaning up against the wall, chatting with another member of the Debbie entourage. I have no idea why the "Foolish Beat" boy was there, or why he was expecting not to get recognized given that MTV was playing the video day and night. Paula and I decided it would be totally cheesy to go talk to him, so it was my job. In one of my all-time low points as a human being, I rushed up and shook his hand. I asked, "Will you give her a present from us?" He rolled his eyes and said, "Uh, *surrrrre*." I gave him the gift bag with our mix tape.

Paula and I went to the bar and toasted Debbie's punk rock

future. The future was incredibly bright. Debbie Gibson was going to go punk rock. Johnny Depp was going to inspire world peace. And there was still enough summer left for me to make a move.

When Paula left town, she left fast. One day I called her house and her housemate told me she was gone. Didn't even know where. I never got to say good-bye, but I would have only said something stupid. The tiny kindnesses that passed between us were real. They were the kind of tiny kindnesses that teach you how to imagine bigger ones. But summer was over. And what about the cast of our little *Dial MTV* soap opera? What happened to the icons who shared our little moment in time?

Debbie Gibson? She never called. Did she ever hear that tape? Of course not. Her next album, *Electric Youth*, was terrible, which surprised exactly two people. She is now a famous Broadway star named Deborah.

George Michael? He eventually came out. This surprised the same two people.

Def Leppard? Their next album was called *Adrenalize*. It had a great song called "Stand Up (Kick Love into Motion)," but no one cared.

The hot boy from the "Foolish Beat" video? He was also in Debbie's "Lost in Your Eyes" video. I don't know if he ever came out, and not even I care.

Cher? Broke up with the hot young Italian stallion who was in that video. Stayed famous, which surprised everyone.

Lita Ford stayed cool and always will be cool. Tiffany put out a great second album that flopped, but I could still sing you most of the songs on it. Axl Rose lost his mojo, Adam Curry cut his hair, and Johnny Depp is still the most important person on the planet every now and then, especially the haircut he had in *What's Eating Gilbert Grape* four years later.

Thanks to all concerned. It was a summer. A year later, there was another one. The world has lots of summers, whether you choose to show up for them or not. This was a huge surprise to both of us.

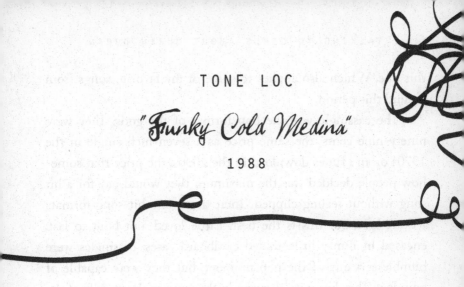

TONE LOC
"Funky Cold Medina"
1988

Why do I love the cassingle? As Whitney herself might say, I don't know why I like it ... I just do!

More and more, my cassingles are the format that rivets this decade into my head. It sums up the Hot Radio explosion of the '80s, all the Latin disco and rap kids coming out of nowhere with 1-900 numbers and a date on *Club MTV* with Downtown Julie Brown. If any objet d'pop lives and dies with this decade, it's this humble little gadget, even though the cassingle survived the '80s and carried the news on into the '90s, especially since releasing a cassingle always remained a very '80s thing to do. If there was ever a format designed to be played once and then thrown away, it's this one. Which also applies to some of my favorite songs from around this period.

The cassingle was the pop format of the gods. They were ninety-nine cents, the same price as a seven-inch single in the 1970s or an iTunes download in the 2000s, the price that somehow people decided was the maximum they would pay for a hit song without feeling clipped. There aren't any hit-song formats I don't love, but this is the best. Little loved, not built to last, encased in flimsy little folded-cardboard cases, cassingles were humble servants of the pop moment, but they were capable of grandeur. They began to show up in the racks in the middle of the 1980s, just as the Walkman and the boom box became the standard playback media; they were gone by the 2000s, when the hard drive took over. But for the years in between, those hardworking little gadgets were the coin of the realm when it came to pop dreams. They were shiny, brittle and cheap, exactly like the songs they delivered.

It's one of those gadgets that gets left behind by history, like the VHS tape, the floppy disk or the rotary phone. But it has its fervent devotees. Like the MP3, it was a push-button mode of temporary pleasures. As seven-inches disappeared, and twelve-inches became iconic cultural documents, cassingles were something that just got stuffed into a shoebox under the bureau. Twelve-inches were for big brothers; cassingles were for little sisters. But the pure no-frills functionality was part of the beauty. It never had the pretensions of the regular CD single, which always seemed like a total waste—one song on a seventy-minute CD?—

or the short-lived and just plain stupid three-inch disc, which required a clumsy little adapter to play. The cassingle was inherently devoid of any artistic aspirations at all. Like any pop format worth its salt, then or now, it was designed for kids on the go, an impulse purchase to be spun a few times on a banged-up Walkman, then thrown away and ash-canned forever.

There was no such thing as a cassingles career. Nobody wanted to look like they put any kind of effort into their cassingles, so the artwork and packaging was shoddy on purpose. But the cassingle could do things with '80s/'90s sonics that neither vinyl nor aluminum singles could do. The glossier, shinier, more treble-driven the production, the more snazzily it adapted to the tight storage capacity. It was designed for flimsy sound, again like the MP3—when you were listening on vinyl or CD, and you heard a hit by Paula Abdul or Fine Young Cannibals, you could hear how screechy and thin the production was. But those beats sounded immense on a cheap little cassingle. It was also designed for rickety careers, which is why most of my most cherished cassingles came from one-hit wonders. They were about fun fun fun. The idea of a culturally significant cassingle is absurd by definition—that was the point.

The cassingle was perfect for teen screams: albums were for grown-ups, and the cassingle was the most anticredibility music gadget ever devised. If you debased your art to cassingles, grown-up CD-player owners wouldn't touch your album. Between 1988 and 1991, the cost of an album basically tripled, and never came back down; the cassingle was the result.

That's probably why it's been scorned and despised through the years. But it's time to hail the noble cassingle. It gave us so much and asked for so little. The cassingle served its technologically appointed purpose in history and then fled into the night. We shall not see its like again.

In honor of the cassingle, a brief shrine to thirty historic favorites, the ones that defined that groovy little piece of plastic. Some I stole from my youngest sister, Caroline. Others I bought for her, then "borrowed" like it was last month's *Sassy*. Some I bought and she stole from me. Who keeps track? They're all scattered around in shoeboxes now, most of them in her basement, where her now five-year-old daughter will no doubt dig them up any day now and ask the questions every mother longs to hear: "Mommy, what was a Bobby Brown? What does 'NKOTB' mean? Why was there a Wild Thing?"

Some of these songs have become eternal classics; most haven't. But none of them were by respectable adult artists, because they avoided these things like the plague. If you're Sting, and you've just recorded a sensitive, jazzy song that rhymes "Mephistopheles" with "autumn breeze," do you want to see it in a fuchsia-and-lime-striped cardboard box with Bubblicious stuck to it? No! Sting liked money, but he didn't like it *that* much.

If you released your song on a cassingle, it's because you were desperate. But that just meant you were trying harder.

Note, the following list contains relics from both the '80s and '90s, so I could show the love to this format's entire spectrum.

Tone Loc, "Funky Cold Medina" (1988)

What the Kingsmen were to the rock-and-roll 45, what Henry Fielding was to the epistolary English novel, what Tim Conway was to the comedy-golf VHS, Tone Loc was to the cassingle. If I were taking a cassingle to a desert island, which admittedly would be kind of stupid, this is the one I would take.

Tone Loc, "Wild Thing" (1988)

Or maybe this one.

Paula Abdul, "Forever Your Girl" (1989)

Long before she became America's favorite not-at-all-drug-crazed judge in a TV singing competition, and don't those days already seem like a dream too good to be true, she just wanted to sing disco ditties about banging cats and chasing coldhearted snakes.

Debbie Gibson, "Foolish Beat" (1988)

There's an actual cover photo: Debbie sitting alone at a restaurant table looking sad because the boy of her dreams stood her up. The flip side has a "Debbie Gibson Mega Mix" medley of "Only in My Dreams," "Shake Your Love" and "Out of the Blue," making this a very special value. I paid three bucks for it, probably the most I ever shelled out for a cassingle.

George Michael, "Monkey" (1988)

I would totally wear that lederhosen ensemble he's rocking in this video. But no way could my calves be as seductive as George Michael's.

Whitney Houston, "So Emotional" (1987)

The one where she sings, "When you talk, I just watch your mouth." We know what that's like, Whitney.

Bobby Brown, "Every Little Step" (1989)

Every girl wanted to be Bobby B's prerogative in 1989. Every boy wanted to be him.

Fine Young Cannibals, "I'm Not the Man I Used to Be" (1989)

If I ever told you that once upon a time, Fine Young Cannibals were cool, you would probably conclude I'd been sipping the angel dust slurpees again, but you'd be wrong. If you were a hipster gal in 1989, you were madly in love with this guy, partly because of his androgynous, post-racial, multicultural looks, but partly also because he sang about girls who drive him crazy (*Whoop! Whoop!*) and he can't help himself.

Young MC, "Bust a Move" (1989)

"You want it, you got it." I loved this one so much, I totally wore out its little cardboard case and relocated it to a full-

size plastic cassette case. Only a handful of cassingles
earn that.

Rick Astley, "It Would Take a Strong Strong Man" (1988)

Everybody knows Rick Astley because of the phenomenon
of "rickrolling." But I remember him fondly because I had a
crush on a girl in Boston who looked a lot like him (and was
a big fan of his, as so many girls mysteriously were). So each
Rick Astley cassingle seemed like another chapter in our
story. First, there was the giddy crush of "Never Gonna Give
You Up," then the deeper longing of "Together Forever."
By the time of this song, Rick's starting to realize it's never
going to work out with this girl, but he still can't move on
because "It Would Take a Strong Strong Man" to ever let her
go. Poor dude—his next hit was "Giving Up on Love." Nobody even noticed when he made an attempted comeback in
the '90s with a new haircut and the self-explanatory "Cry for
Help." Jesus, I sure hope he met somebody.

Neneh Cherry, "Buffalo Stance" (1989)

At the same time as the above crush, I also kind of liked her
best friend—it was the by-no-means rare circumstance of
crushing out on two girls who are friends and not being sure
which one you want to make a move on, so they both slip
away. This song was playing in the bar the night she told me
that if you can peel the whole Bud label off in one piece, it
means you're a virgin.

Soul II Soul, "Keep on Movin'" (1989)

This song is surprisingly obscure today, but it's the ultimate fusion of London hip-hop, Caribbean reggae, Philly soul and California new wave—a cultural event that only could have happened on a cassingle.

Blackstreet, "No Diggity" (1996)

I stole this one from my mom, who got it as a Christmas gift from one of her students. Note: my mom was teaching first grade at the time! Damn! I liked my first grade teacher too, but I never gave her a song about a hooker who got game by the pound.

Jellybean with Elisa Fiorillo, "Who Found Who" (1988)

This disco bopper was the first time I noticed that a single had obviously been produced with the cassingle consumer in mind—it sounded flat and lifeless as a twelve-inch, but totally perky on tape. Not a huge hit, but a technological pivot point.

Sir Mix-A-Lot, "Baby Got Back" (1992)

The only hit song of the cassingle era (of my lifetime, actually) that literally everybody can quote at will. As far as I can tell, this is the most famous song on earth. Any English speaker under the age of eighty can rap at least a few lines from this song. My nieces and nephews know it from *Shrek*. I am not aware of any Beatles song to achieve this level of cultural saturation.

Sophie B. Hawkins, "Damn I Wish I Was Your Lover" (1992)
This song is still in rotation anywhere music is played, even though it was never on a hit album and never got any airplay as a video. It was just pure cassingle consciousness, distilled to its essence.

Milli Vanilli, "Blame It on the Rain" (1989)
My sister Caroline had this theory that the Milli Vanilli hits were a continuous soap opera. First they meet the girl ("Girl You Know It's True"), then they beg her not to dis them ("Baby Don't Forget My Number"), then they break up ("Girl I'm Gonna Miss You"), until finally accepting their fate ("Blame It on the Rain"). I totally buy this theory. Rob and Fab did this at Ricky Schroeder's birthday party on *Silver Spoons*. Personally, I think Milli Vanilli should be honored as a fantastic pop scam instead of demonized over some silly lip-synching scandal. Some blame their producer, some blame the media, but I, like Rob and Fab, prefer to blame it on the rain.

Ralph Tresvant, "Sensitivity" (1990)
The only New Edition guy who never became a huge solo star, but the one who made the finest cassingle.

Kon Kan, "I Beg Your Pardon" (1989)
I defy you to name another era that could produce a Canadian disco group who could rip off New Order, sample a vin-

tage country classic, do the rock, do the freak, and then have
the decency to disappear as soon as the song is done.

Kris Kross, "Jump" (1992)

It's only in the past few years I've noticed the existence of
people who are too cool to like this song. They will all wither,
blow away in the wind and drift to the sea, where the waves
will be singing along with Kris Kross.

Kris Kross, "Warm It Up" (1992)

Like *The Godfather: Part II*, a sequel that tops the original.
"Warm it up, Kris! I'm about to! Warm it up, Kris! 'Cause
that's what I was born to do!" (Beavis: "What were *we* born
to do?" Butt-Head: "Uuuuh . . . I don't know.")

Corina, "Temptation" (1991)

She wears handcuffs on the cover, symbolizing her enslave-
ment by the addictions she sings about, whether it's sex
or cassingles. I also bought the twelve-inch and the entire
Corina album, but it's this item I still play.

Londonbeat, "I've Been Thinking About You" (1991)

Fine Young Cannibals took too long to come up with a
follow-up, so Londonbeat moved in. You still hear this one
sometimes, usually in the supermarket. The cassingle cover
photo has the members of this band with chins in palms and

eyebrows furrowed—they are *thinking*. Side 2 is a medley of album tracks.

Kristine W, "One More Try" (1996)
The guy who cuts my hair now is one of her friends, so I get to hear gossip about her all the time now. He is *never* surprised I know who she is.

Biz Markie, "Just a Friend" (1989)
One of the truly classic cassingle covers: Biz is holding a handkerchief to wipe away his tears, although he makes sure his handkerchief doesn't cover up his gold dookie rope. And that's why he's the Biz.

Tiffany, "All This Time" (1988)
I bought this at a flea market a couple years ago, from a grizzled bastard with Dewar's breath who was selling cassingles out of a shoebox for three bucks. I was aghast—ninety-nine cents max! But I really wanted this, and unlike doves, cassingle fans have no pride, so I talked him down to two bucks. But every time I play this, I still get mad about it.

Caroline and Kerry, "Twist and Shout" (1989)
My sister and one of her girlfriends recorded this at the make-your-own-tape booth at the mall. What ever happened to those make-your-own-tape booths? They didn't last long, but they were such a big deal at the time—for fifty cents, you

could record your own karaoke cassingle. As far as I know, Sonic Youth's Kim Gordon was the only rock star to release one of these on an album ("Addicted to Love"), but naturally, I prefer the sound of two screamy Irish girls.

Usher, "You Make Me Wanna" (1997)

One Saturday morning, I heard this song on MTV and immediately drove to the mall to buy it. The girl at the counter sang it as she rang it up. Usher's album didn't even exist yet—he may be the last historic example of an artist who broke via tape.

Somethin' for the People, "My Love Is the Shhh!" (1997)

I first heard this on MTV the same day as "You Make Me Wanna," and bought it at the same time, but Usher's the one who got famous. Sorry, Somethin' for the People! Three months after this R & B slow jam dominated the airwaves, it was gone and forgotten permanently, and I haven't heard it on the radio once since. But it was damn good, and if it weren't for my cassingle copy, it basically wouldn't even exist in my world. I guess it's the People's loss!

Billie Ray Martin, "Your Loving Arms" (1995)

Late in the game, purchased with love and ardor from the used-tape rack at Plan 9 Records. It cost me a quarter. It was 1999, four years after the song came and went and long after the rest of the world had forgotten it, and I was grateful to find proof it ever existed. I also found Alison Krauss's huge 1995 country hit "Baby, Now That I've Found You," and on the drive home, I gave them both elegiac spins in the car. It sounded like cassingles were saying good-bye, and indeed they were—they had entered their pity-retail phase.

But the glory of these songs summed up why the cassingle was solid gold, in that plastic kind of way.

I had already heard ... the Baby, Now That I've Found You", and on the other three ...

But the quality of these songs suffered ... the example ...

NEW KIDS ON THE BLOCK

"Hangin' Tough"

1989

In the spring of 1989, I was the stacks manager at Harvard's Cabot Library. In librarian jargon, a stacks manager is a tall guy who puts heavy books in high places. The word "manager" doesn't mean that I had anyone under me. (In fact, the lack of anybody under me was a problem all year, but that's another issue.) I loved my work at the library. It was a long winter and a cold spring and I spent most of my hours in the underground stacks shelving books about biology in the HQ section, grooving to my Walkman. I was in the second year of what turned out to be a longer year of celibacy than I'd planned. You remember the George Michael song about sex, the one that goes, "Sex is natural, sex is fun, sex is best when it's one on one"? I wondered if maybe George Michael was only half right: sex is best when it's one.

At this time I was heavily involved in trading tapes with my little sister Caroline, whose Catholic middle school class had just voted her "Most Daring" and "Most Awesome." For her thirteenth birthday party, she had the whole basement packed with the girls in her class, and led them all in a chant: "We hate boys! Except the New Kids! On the Block!" She meant it too. Caroline was heavily involved in stalking the New Kids on the Block, who were still mainly a local Boston phenomenon. She wrote an essay for school on the topic of the "Person I Most Admire," and picked Joey McIntyre.

Unfortunately, I no longer have my copy of this essay, since I made the mistake of giving it to her husband as a gift, whereupon Caroline grabbed it and ripped it to shreds. She has informed all her siblings that none of her four adorable children are ever allowed to know how much their mom loved the New Kids on the Block. This has something to do with the fact that it violates the fourth commandment against worshipping graven images (and that Donnie Wahlberg sure was graven). So my lips are sealed. Sydney, if you're reading, put this book down now! *Dora*'s on! Go!

Caroline was the ultimate badass baby sister. She did not really have the neuroses that afflicted her big brother. In fact, she wasn't frightened of anything. We big kids never stayed out all night or raised hell or stalked pop stars. We had no idea being badass was even an option. Our parents were infuriatingly trusting, so we never got to outrage them. They never gave us any curfew, so we never stayed out late. They never locked up their liquor, so it never occurred to us to sneak any of it. If we felt like cutting school, they'd just shrug and say "fine," so what was the point? It drove us crazy.

But Caroline? She got away with the things that older siblings never even imagine. Believe me, none of us ever told one another to "fuck off" at the dinner table. Saying "fuck off" at dinner, with my mom sitting right there, would have been like kneeling before the Holy Inquisition and using my tongue to fold the communion wafer into a paper airplane. But when Caroline told Tracey to "fuck off," all Mom did was make Caroline write up a list of twenty-five things she should have said instead. Caroline's list of twenty-five "fuck off" alternatives began strong, but by the end she was struggling—the final two items she came up with were "Forsake me" and "Begone." "Forsake me!" is still a popular conversation-ender in our sibling circle.

My sisters and I were shocked. None of us dared to say "frickin'" or "stupid" or "douchebag" at home. Not even "d-bag," which I tried once. We sure screwed up by getting born so early, when our folks had so much more energy.

Caz and I always traded tapes, trying to turn each other on to the music we loved. I taped her the Replacements and the Ramones; she taped me Bon Jovi and Tiffany. I taped her *Let It Be* for her birthday. (Conscientious big brother that I am, I omitted "Gary's Got a Boner.") We liked each other's music way more than we would admit. Bon Jovi's "Wild in the Streets" stopped me dead in my tracks, a stupid-rock mall anthem to end all mall anthems, to end all anthems, to end all malls. Meanwhile, Caroline was putting the Replacements' "Sixteen Blue" on her answering machine. Whenever we confessed how much we loved each other's music, we each felt both flattered and disappointed at the same time.

Caroline made me a tape for my birthday that winter, when I turned twenty-three. According to the note she wrote inside the case, "This is dedicated to the men in my life—Jordan, Rob, Jon, Joe, Danny, & Donnie." "Rob" is me. The other five are the New Kids on the Block. It's called *Rob's Cultural Experience*, and it has her narrating between the songs to explain the significance of why Bobby Brown is a genius or why Lita Ford kicks ass.

Caroline was really the only person on earth I could talk to about girls. That sounds weird, since she was only twelve, but she was always braver and bolder than I was, and did her best to teach me basic social skills. She could always be counted on to say, "Who needs girls? You have me." She wore her hair pouffed up like Joan Jett in the video for "I Hate Myself for Loving You." She wore a black leather jacket to play up her resemblance to Joan. Hell, she even took "Joan" as her confirmation name.

The New Kids were starting to blow up across the country, the way New Edition and Bobby Brown did a few years earlier. Caroline was plugged into the Catholic schoolgirl grapevine that knew exactly where they were at any given moment, allowing her to lead packs of her friends in chasing them down the street. She knew about it every time one of her friends had a friend who had a friend who saw them buying condoms at the Osco Drug in

Dorchester. Her favorites were Joey and Donnie. She met Donnie once backstage and he gave her a kiss on the cheek. For months, she answered the phone, "Donnie kissed me!"

One day, Caroline was telling me Joey Mac stories and she mentioned that his nickname in high school was "Wedgie." It only made her love him more fiercely. There was always something humble and lovable about those New Kids. They never had the disastrous post-teen-pop crash. After the hits dried up, they got on with their lives. My friend Desiree even went on a New Kids cruise last winter, where you'd call room service and Donnie or Jordan would show up at your cabin with your food.

Caroline made me another excellent tape that winter where she actually interviewed the New Kids. She did this by asking questions into the mike, and then sticking in a line from a song as the answer.

CAROLINE:
"Do you have something to tell me?"

JOEY MCINTYRE:
"Please don't go, girl! You're my best friend! You're my everything!"

She orchestrates the whole tape as a news report ("This is Caroline Sheffield on WNOB, live from Dorchester") about a rumble between the New Kids and Lita Ford, "the self-proclaimed First Lady of Rock." Obviously, Lita kicks all their asses. The New Kids ask Lita, "What'cha Gonna Do About It?" Lita answers with a line from "Under the Gun": "Now the time has come, it's your turn to die." The rumble gets messy, with rock stars from other tapes joining in: Ozzy, Poison, Public Enemy. I have to say, Caroline sure goes overboard creating all this dialogue.

AXL ROSE (from "One in a Million"):
"Hey man, won't you cut me some slack?"

NEW KIDS (from "Hangin' Tough"):
"We ain't gonna cut anybody any slack!"

She even gets the Psychedelic Furs in the mix, with one word from the *Pretty in Pink* title song.

CAROLINE:
"Joey, what is the name of your girlfriend?"

JOEY:
"Caroline."

These days, she mostly listens to Taylor Swift, because that's what her toddlers are into. Sydney and Jack play a game where they take turns pretending to be Taylor; one sings "White Horse" while the other cheers and claps, then they trade places. The music changes, I guess, but the fan gene is a dominant one.

We still argue about music, because we love the argument too much to give it up. It's always going to be one of our ways of talking to each other. She still loves the Replacements, so much that she actually buys Tommy Stinson's solo albums, even though I urge her not to. A couple of Christmases ago, she gave me an autographed copy of Paul Westerberg's solo album, which she got waiting in line at a Boston in-store signing. Needless to say, she was the only girl who showed up, plus the only person under thirty. It knocked me out to see her photos, posing with Paul Westerberg— two people who taught me so much about courage and not being afraid of life and going on your nerve, two soul confidants who got me through some grim times. It made me feel guilty for not liking the record, so I forced myself to play it until I liked it.

Paul Westerberg has a big crazy smile in the picture, with his arm around Caroline. He obviously didn't get a lot of girls asking for pictures. He looks real happy to see her.

"Ain't No Half Steppin'"

1989

I was twenty-three and living with my grandfather, just because he was ninety and by himself and I wanted to spend time with him while I could. Ever since my grandmother died in 1986, he'd lived alone in the three-decker in Forest Hills, an Irish neighborhood in Boston. I would take the T home every night and he'd cook us steaks, and we'd listen to the Irish folk music on WROL as he smoked his pipe and told stories about the railroad.

He'd lived in this house since 1933, when he and Nana got married. They came over separately in 1924, after growing up on dirt farms in Ireland, and got good jobs in America, she as a maid, he as a brake inspector on the New Haven Railroad. After he retired from the railroad, he was a security guard in a department store, and then in the Gardner Museum in the Fenway. He wor-shipped FDR and was active in his union. Every time he tried retiring, my grandmother would send him back out to work. She was deaf, but she wasn't *that* deaf. And the man could talk.

They'd courted for nine years, as she'd always dreamed she'd eventually go back to County Kerry, whereas he was determined never to go back to County Cork again. As a little kid, I asked him if he ever missed the farm, and he said, "My boy, I was so glad to be off the farm I didn't know I was working." He didn't get to emigrate until he was twenty-four because he had to wait until his elder brother got married. In accordance with tradition, his brother got the farm and he got the brother's wedding dowry, which he spent on a boat ticket to America. Those two weeks on the boat were the happiest days of his life up to that point. Amer-ica had a railroad, where he only had to work sixteen hours a day. This was the life. He was terrified that any of his grandchildren might someday move back, after all the trouble it took him to get out. In the sixty-five years since he emigrated, he'd only gone back once, to settle the estate (i.e., give the farm away to the neighbors) when his brother died in 1968. He told my uncle Gerard, "There was fuck all there when I left, and there's fuck all there now."

Every night, when I came home from work, I would hear him halfway down Craft Place yelling at the Red Sox on his TV set. "Come on, Ellis! Do it for your ancestors!" His favorite Red Sox player was Ellis Burks, who he called "The Irishman." He loved to yell at Ellis about the glory of his Celtic name and the tradition of Irish sportsmen. "Think it for your ancestors, Ellis! Sure they had to hit it with a hurley, but you have a bat!" Ellis Burks is black, by the way. After my grandfather died in 1991, I went to County Cork and visited the cabin where he was born, and left an Ellis Burks baseball card there.

Some of my friends, when I told them I was rooming with my grandfather, assumed I was taking care of him, helping him go to the bathroom, stuff like that. These people have never met an old Irish guy. He wouldn't even let me take him shopping. He would take the bus in by himself without telling me. When I got home and found out he'd been gallivanting alone on the bus at his age, I would blow a gasket and yell at him, while he sat in his easy chair laughing at me. He walked with a cane, but he just liked how it looked.

After the baseball game, he would cook us a steak and tell stories. Then we trooped out to the living room for *Sanford and Son*, a show we'd been watching together my entire life. He could relate to Fred Sanford. They were both cantankerous old men who wore cardigans and overalls. Both were widowers who liked to hear themselves talk. They were exiles with thick accents—Fred Sanford a St. Louis man in L.A., my grandfather a County Cork immigrant in Boston—bewildered by normal Americans. All the people around them who were at ease in the new world—these people all seemed as ridiculous as the white cop who tells Fred Sanford "right up" when he means "right on." Being old and far from home was a joke my grandfather got.

After he went to bed, I'd stay up and watch *Yo! MTV Raps* for my fix of De La Soul and Big Daddy Kane and Public Enemy.

I would switch it back to the Eternal Word Network so he could get the first of his seven daily Masses. If I forgot to change the station back, we'd have the same conversation about it. "I got your jokers this morning," he said. That meant he'd turned on the TV expecting Mass and got *Club MTV* or *Remote Control*.

When he tried watching MTV with me, he found it hilarious. The one tape of mine he liked, oddly enough, was the Smiths. His favorite was "Please, Please, Please Let Me Get What I Want." He said, "At least that's got a bit of an air to it."

He preferred the radio in the kitchen, which would sing him the songs of the old country, even though when he was my age, he couldn't wait to get out of the old country. The songs would remind him of other songs, and he'd sometimes close his eyes to recite. *One two three, balance like me. Now you're a fairy, you've got your own faults.* Some of the songs were from Ireland, some were from America. Some were American pop songs about the Irish. Some were Irish songs about coming to America and getting lost. *Your right foot is crazy, your left foot is lazy, but don't be un-aizy, I'll teach you to waltz.*

Irish songs make you feel a little nostalgic for the old country, even if it wasn't the country where you were born. When Nana was alive, she would "go to Ireland" in the evenings, just sit with the lights out for an hour or two, dreaming that she was back on the farm. Then she'd get up and do her devotions around the apartment, with a Vermont Maid bottle full of holy water. She would walk around the apartment flinging it in all directions. To the south, for Uncle Eddie in Brazil. To the other directions, where her other children lived. All over my grandfather and me. Every object in the apartment being fairly damp and extremely holy, she had done her work for the night. Now that she was gone, he and I were alone with just the songs and the time to talk. So we talked.

Or, rather, he talked. When my mom was growing up, he was a silent man, but one day in 1961, he was given the job of riding up and down the Eastern seaboard with a couple of new engineers from the Philippines. Their English wasn't good, so his job was explaining to them patiently and in detail every aspect of the train operation. He started talking that day and never stopped. So we sat in the kitchen and listened to the radio. He would sing songs about the old country and lecture me about men he idolized (FDR, Eamon de Valera, Cardinal Cushing) and men he despised (Ronald Reagan, Richard Nixon, Cardinal Law).

One night, I came downstairs to say goodnight. He was sitting in the kitchen with his shoes off, and he looked unusually anxious. He was holding a pair of nail clippers. His toenails were ingrown and giving him pain. "It's the age," he said. He couldn't reach down and cut them himself.

I thought, no problem, and got down on my knees in front of his chair. But I was not prepared for blood. As soon as I began cutting the toenails, blood started gushing from his feet. The skin under the nail cracked. I'm usually not squeamish at the sight of blood, but this was my grandfather I was cutting up.

"It doesn't hurt," he kept saying. "Please keep going."

He'd asked my uncle to do this job a couple of Christmases

ago. My uncle gave it a go, but the blood freaked him out too—this was his father, after all—and he only got one foot done before he had to beg off the other one. I knew it must have mortified my grandfather to ask my uncle for help with something this intimate, and I knew he was afraid I would say no. I steeled myself and forced myself through it. I kept telling myself, "It's just blood. My grandfather's blood. Blood that carried him across an ocean and is in my veins too and *okaaaay* it's just blood. It doesn't hurt. His body will make more. He won't bleed to death. Nobody dies from getting their toenails cut."

"Keep going, boy."

"Nobody ever *has* died from this. He won't be the first. I'm totally not killing him, and if I am, I'm sure my mom will believe me when I say that it was his idea and that I ignored my own best judgment when a ninety-year-old man told me to bleed him. That's what's happening. I'm bleeding him and I am a fucking butcher."

I had one foot done. There was blood all over my hands. I asked permission to towel him off, and wrapped up his left foot in a dishrag. Was this normal, to do this for old people? I wouldn't know if it was normal. I had no idea what his blood type was, or if he knew, or what I'd do if this really was a bad idea.

But it wasn't a bad idea. "Tell me when you need me to do this again," I said. "Don't let them grow this long." I figured he'd never ask again, but he did, in just a couple weeks.

He also tore an ad out from the Sunday paper to mail away for a tiny little pair of nail scissors. He wrote a check for $3.50 and asked me to drop it in the mail. "And how are the nails doing?" I asked. "Would you like me to clip them tonight?" He said, aaaah, no, which meant it was now something he wanted me to cajole him into, so he wouldn't have to ask. It was a lonely ritual. It was the first time I ever felt I had to keep a secret from my mom about my grandfather. As soon as I mentioned blood, it would be a big deal. So I didn't tell anyone. It was just my hands, his feet, his blood, our secret, and it would be this way from now on. Even after I moved out, every time I came to visit, I was asking him about his feet, and talking him into it, the way I had to talk him into letting me drive him to Atlas Liquors for a bit of the Jameson. The way he used to talk me into taking money when I would come visit.

Jesus, Irish men. We can't ask for a goddamn thing, can we? Asking for help, or accepting it, we just can't handle it, can we? What the hell is wrong with us and how did we get this way?

He kept asking about the scissors he sent away for, even though they were no different from the scissors I got at the drugstore. The only way they were any different is that when these arrived in the mail, it would mean he had gotten them on his own, with no help from me. But they didn't arrive. He wrote the scissors people a reminder letter and asked me to mail it for him. I wrote my own letter and slipped it into the same envelope. It wasn't as polite as my grandfather's, because I was angry. Even as I was writing it, I could tell it was my mother writing, the furious kind of letter my mom used to write our teachers and principals. It was the letter she would have written if she'd known about the toenails or the scissors. I wrote that if they needed to steal $3.50 from an old man, they were welcome to it but they were assholes. The scissors arrived the following week.

Late at night, kneeling on my grandfather's kitchen floor, I cut into his skin again and felt him flinch. My hands were bloody. On my knees, on the floor, doing the bloody work of love. Learning, over and over. The work of love will make you bloody and it will make you lonely.

L'TRIMM

"Cars with the Boom"

1989

The first time I watched *The Wraith*, I was with a girl. It was the greatest '80s teen-trash melodrama I'd ever seen, which was probably because I was watching it with a girl. Renee was doing her regular Friday night babysitting gig out in Batesville, and although I'd only been her boyfriend for a few weeks, I had graduated to the status of the boy who shows up to distract the babysitter. I'd been waiting for this a long time. Mr. and Mrs. Sorrell had a well-stocked refrigerator and cable TV, both of which were novelties for a couple of starving grad students in Charlottesville. So, as soon as little Lindsey was asleep, we killed a box of Chicken in a Biskit crackers, drank Rolling Rocks and watched some trashy movies. A plush couch that was bigger than my apartment? Awesome! A refrigerator full of beer? Awesome! *The Wraith*? Mmmm, cancel that order of awesomes.

It's a new-wave soap opera set in a small town in Arizona, with Sherilyn Fenn as the all-American beach bunny, plus the perverse twist that she's a beach bunny in the middle of the desert, where the swimming hole has to be dug with bulldozers. Charlie Sheen is the mysterious new kid in town, who was secretly her true love in his past life. Except he was viciously killed by this evil gang of biker pirates who rampage wildly on the highways, so he's come back to earth from outer space to get vengeance on the bikers, claim Sherilyn for himself, and drive this really cool, huge, black Wraithmobile, which is like a spaceship on wheels. The biker pirates have leather jackets and names like Skank or Og, but they can't handle Charlie Sheen.

"It's a wraith!" splutters Skank, trying to explain it to the other bad guys in their underground hideout. "A wraith, man! A ghost! An evil spirit, and it ain't cool!"

We loved every minute of this deplorable film, even though practically every scene in this movie comes from *Rebel Without a Cause*, *Purple Rain*, or some other teen-outlaw biker flick. Randy Quaid plays the sheriff trying to solve the mystery, but like everybody else in this town, he's never seen a TV movie before, so he has no idea Charlie Sheen is the Wraith. The soundtrack is the essence of '80s electro-blare: Billy Idol's "Rebel Yell," Nick Gilder's "Scream of Angels," Ozzy's "Secret Loser." It's a star-crossed romance for sure, because while Charlie might be from out in the great blue yonder, Sherilyn is wearing a red bikini, and this girl is definitely flesh and blood. She works at the roadside drive-in burger joint as a roller-girl waitress, which means she skates through the parking lot shaking her ass to Robert Palmer's "Addicted to Love." She's literally sex on wheels, a spaceboy's dream girl with wide rock-and-roll hips and a foxy ankle bracelet. But she can't figure out why she's so drawn to Charlie Sheen, gosh darn it. Why does he remind her of somebody she used to know, like the boy who was killed by the biker gang? And where did Charlie get those mysterious scars on his back? Hmmmmmm!

"Are we not supposed to know Charlie Sheen is like an E.T.?" Renee asked.

"No, I think we're supposed to know. But Sherilyn doesn't know."

"Is she a moron?"

"She's never seen a wraith before."

"She just switched from a red bikini to a blue bikini. That means she's totally going to do him."

"If she does him and she still doesn't notice he's from outer space, she's got big problems."

"She's got big something. Look at those! She's wearing that to work!"

"I'm worried about these two," I said, rummaging for crumbs at the bottom of the cracker box. "It's time for them to make out but we've already heard 'Rebel Yell.' Maybe if they didn't make out during 'Rebel Yell' they missed their shot."

"No way. She's too hot. No boy is from that far outer space."

They share their first kiss on his motorcycle, while a Bonnie

Tyler ballad plays on the soundtrack. Then Charlie kills practically everybody in town except for Sherilyn, and that's when our hero confesses his secret identity to the flesh-and-blood girl he left behind on earth. He can't stay on this planet, but he's returned to carry her off into the stars with him. Charlie tells Sherilyn, "I've come a long ways for you." She cannot resist the Wraith. The movie ends with Sherilyn on the back of Charlie's motorcycle as we watch their taillights fade.

For some reason, I started sobbing at the end of *The Wraith* and couldn't stop. I'd never cried in front of Renee before, much less at a Charlie Sheen movie, and I felt like an idiot. But she was completely cool about it. As the credits rolled, she patted me on the back and mused, "Sherilyn has a nice ass, doesn't she?" At that moment, I knew she was the girl for me. Of course, we'd already been going out for a few weeks, so I wasn't, like, shocked or anything. But still, it's never not nice to keep realizing.

I was somebody's boyfriend now. This would mean a lot of trial and error. But she was who I wanted to try and err with.

Our first fall together, we did a lot of aimless driving around in the countryside. We'd cruise by the Amoco Food Shoppe on Route 29 for some chicken-battered french fries and hit the open road. When I say "aimless," I do not mean anything negative— "aimless" was the major achievement of my life so far. Who needs aims, anyway? I'd spent twenty-three years collecting aims, and now I was sitting on so many I couldn't give them away. Aimless was something I was just learning. So I kept telling myself how lucky I was to learn it from her, and kept praying I wouldn't get carsick in her '78 LeBaron as she whipped around the hills. No doubt you've heard the expression "She drove it like she stole it?" This girl drove it like she stole it from the cops and then did donuts on the altar of the Basilica of the Holy Redeemer on Mission Hill. That's how she drove it.

We'd listen to hip-hop, which was all new to her. She'd never gotten into it before, and so she gobbled up my hip-hop cassettes. Her favorites were the women rappers like Roxanne Shante, MC Lyte, and L'Trimm, who were two badass Miami teenagers who liked the cars that go boom. Their names were Lady Tigra and Bunny D, and they only valued two things in a man, bass and booty, especially the former. "Cars with the Boom" was about rolling around in the Miami streets with your top down and the woofers exploding, but she thought it was excellent for zooming down the Blue Ridge Parkway. She'd always chant along. "We like the cars! The cars that go boom! We're Tigra and Bunny! And we like the boom!"

Some afternoons she let me drive her around, which was a special occasion. I borrowed my sister Tracey's cherry-red Ford Granada, which she hated because it couldn't do more than forty without shaking all over like the girl in an Eddie Money song. This piece-of-crap Yankee car didn't even have a gun rack. This car did *not* have boom. I secretly thought I was a better driver than she was, but it was just that I was a city driver and she was a country driver. She laughed at me for getting winded on mountain roads at forty-five degree angles, but that's nothing compared with the way she panicked the first time I took her to Boston and drove her down the Arborway.

"There are no lines on this road!" she screamed.

"The lines are in my mind."

"Where are we going?"

"Remember, this is Boston and everyone on the road is a lunatic. Relax."

"I still don't see any lines."

"They don't give you a license here if you notice lines."

"They're not letting you in."

"I'm feeling my way in."

"I hate it. I hate it, hate it, hate it. Now what in God's name is that thing?"

"It's called a rotary."

"You can't be serious."

I took an extra couple of loops around the rotary just for fun, and just to hear her scream like a crazed old Southern lady. She actually said, "Great time of day!" I never heard her yell that one again.

I had never gotten the hang of dating—I was always going to be somebody who either had a girlfriend or didn't. To me, dating was like the scene in *The French Connection* where Gene Hackman is shadowing the perp, Fernando Rey. Gene follows him into the subway. Fernando gets on the train, Gene gets on the train. Fernando gets off, Gene gets off. Back on, the doors close, but Fernando jams his umbrella in the door, so the doors open. Back out, back in, back out, the train pulls out of the station, Fernando waves good-bye through the window, Gene's stuck standing on the platform. There's your date. At least Gene didn't have to pay for it.

But now I was actually on the train with the girl, and for the first time, I felt like we were going somewhere. She'd had millions of boyfriends, so she would get a little impatient at having to tell me all the time that she was *not* being annoying. She was just being a girlfriend. She thought she was doing me a huge favor by explaining to me what girlfriends were like.

"I'm gonna tell you a secret about women," Renee told me one Saturday night after we'd stayed up at least two bourbons and two Bowie albums too late.

"I heard this one before."

"No, this one's different. It's a secret, I promise. There are two kinds of women. The women who'd rather get their way, and women who'd rather get the credit for getting their way. This is the secret: we're all the second kind."

"But you always get your way."

"No, you just keep telling me I always get my way. I like that better than actually getting my way."

"Well, you like to get your way *and* get the credit."

"I do like that, don't I. And I like you."

"Thank you."

"And you know how to freshen a girl's drink."

"We're out of ice."

She loved ordering me to beat people up for her. She didn't want me to *mean* it; she just wanted to me to say, sure honey, even though she knew I couldn't bust the proverbial grape in a fruit fight.

When Renee died in 1997, I could no longer fantasize about

beating up people who were mean to her. It was like Lord Byron asked: "Let the object of affection be snatched away by death, and how is all the pain ever inflicted on them avenged?" Good question. After she died, she left her pain in the world, and I couldn't protect her from it anymore. But then, I never could. I'd come a long way for her. And now I was somewhere new. From the start, I had to realize how helpless I was to protect her from her pain, and the longer we stayed together, the more I felt swamped with awareness of all the bad shit in the world from which I could not protect her.

When Renee had trouble at her day job, she kept a Robin Ventura baseball card on her desk. When steam came out of her ears, she would look at Robin Ventura and think, "Don't charge the mound. Once you agree to fight, you lost already. Don't start none, won't be none." It calmed her down, reminded her to keep her head. To anybody just passing by her desk, it looked like an innocent baseball card of the White Sox third baseman, a handsome jock, nothing more. But to her, it was a coded message, and it had to do with Robin charging the mound when Nolan Ryan hit him in 1993, and how a pitcher on a mound always has the first-punch advantage and it was a total no-win display of temper, even though he was right. Being right is no advantage in the fight—if anything, it's a piano on your back, making you pitifully easy to put in a headlock. When Renee would feel her temperature rising, she would whisper the name to herself, "Robin Ventura," over and over, and usually it would go away. Also, Robin Ventura had a righteous ass, which probably was also partly why she kept the baseball card.

Not being able to protect her from things was the most frightening thing I'd ever felt, and it kicked in as soon as we got together. With every year we spent together, I became more conscious that I now had an infinitely expanding number of reasons to be afraid. I had something to lose. You know the movie *Swamp Thing*? The mad scientist takes Adrienne Barbeau hostage shortly after her topless scene and uses her as bait to entrap the Swamp Thing. When the trap works, the mad scientist gives an evil laugh at the Swamp Thing and says, "The man who loves gives hostages to fortune."

It was lonely, grappling with all those fears. Did all adult people worry about this? I didn't know.

One Sunday afternoon, Renee and I ran out of gas in the middle of a fight, driving across Afton Mountain in my sister's Granada. That car couldn't claim to have a lot of road-worthy virtues, but it did have a functioning gas gauge, and I really should have noticed that the needle was on empty, except Renee and I were too busy sniping at each other about some topic that seemed incredibly important at the time. I honestly don't even remember what it was we were mad about. The car stalled out and I nosed into the breakdown lane. We really wanted to sit in the car and keep fighting, but instead, we got out of the car to fight about which one of us would have to walk down the mountain in search of the nearest gas station.

We stood out there on the side of the road, leaning against the car, both of us staring bleakly at the traffic rushing by us. We began to understand how stupid we were to stay together. Neither of us said a word—we just stood there, our shirts flapping in the breeze like a couple of rags tied to the antenna. We were going to have to use our brains, but it was our brains that got us up here, so something else had to get us down. Is there anyone stupider, weaker, more helpless, but especially stupider, than two twenty-three-year-old kids in love?

Not stupid for running out of gas or even for fighting, but for staying together in the first place. That was the first moment I realized how fucked we were. For the rest of my life, I would have reasons to be afraid. I now had something in my blood stronger and meaner than I was. Two people leaning against a '76 Granada by the side of the road, arms folded, staring at the gravel—this was a posture we could stay in forever, and nobody could protect us from it except each other. Like the Turk says in *The Godfather*, blood is a big expense.

As we stood there, I knew what "hostages to fortune" meant. Love can do whatever it wants to you. And it's a lot meaner than you are. (And then love starts talking to you the way Kirk Douglas talks to Jane Greer in *Out of the Past*.) It won't be quick. I'll break you first. You won't be able to answer the phone or walk around in your own apartment without wondering, is this it? And when it does come, it still won't be quick. And it won't be pretty.

I'm not sure how long we stood there. A car pulled into the breakdown lane ahead of us. It was Renee's friend Becky from Waynesboro, another paralegal in her office. Becky rolled down her driver's-side window. "Yooo-hoooo!" she yelled. "Y'all look like you're in a bit of a pickle." She laughed a bit, then drove off to get us some gas.

"I'll be right back," she hollered before she peeled out. "You two don't go anywhere!"

It took her about twenty minutes. But she came back with a can of gas from the station down the other side of the mountain. Becky taught me how to open a hood and pour gas from a can directly onto a carburetor, a skill I have never used again. Renee and I didn't tell her we'd been fighting. Becky probably guessed.

We thanked her and told her we didn't know what we would have done without her (that was true). She said, "Have a good night," and we said, "We will" (that was a lie).

We nosed back onto Route 250 in silence and defeat. It took a few miles for Renee to turn on the radio again. I didn't want to hear it.

"Come on," she said. "I'm sorry."

"I'm sorry too. I just don't want to talk."

"Smile?"

"Not now."

"Come on. You know I love this song. Rox-ANNE!"

"I don't feel like it."

"Rox-ANNE!"

Pffff. Teeth still clenched. Slow exhale.

"Don't leave me hanging from the Roxanne tree, darlin'. RAAAK-ZAAAAN!"

"Put on a red light."

"That's it! Rox-ANNNE!"

"Purrron uuuh RED! LYYYYY!"

"Yeah! Roxanne!"

"Purrron uuuh REEEEEH! LYYYYY!"

"Roxanne!"

"You don't have to PURRRON UUUH REEEH! LYYYYY!"

"Roxanne!"

Miles go by, no red lights at all.

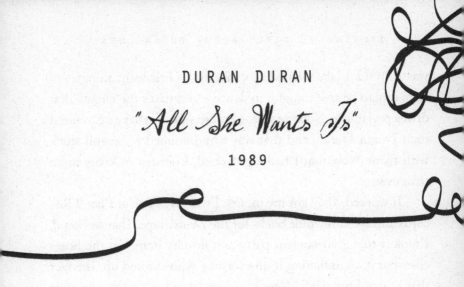

DURAN DURAN
"All She Wants Is"
1989

Duran Duran celebrated the end of the 1980s by releasing their greatest hits album, which they called *Decade*. This was either their way of making fun of Neil Young, exactly the kind of old-school rock idol they had no use for, or their way of reminding everybody they'd stuck around five times as long as anyone expected. I thought I was Duran Duran's biggest fan, but I never dreamed they'd still be making hits in 1989.

"All She Wants Is" was their answer to "I Know What Boys Like." They sang, "All she wants is, all she wants is"—but they wouldn't say what she wants! Duran Duran knew, they just wouldn't tell me. That wasn't fair. George Michael wasn't coy about what the girl wanted from him (she wanted money) and neither was Billy Idol (she wanted mo, mo, mo). Girls want things—to have fun, to be free tonight, to dance—and that's the engine that drives pop music. Nobody seemed more sure of what girls wanted than Duran Duran, and that was why I seemed to be still stuck with them. Now that I had a girlfriend, I needed to know more than ever.

It worked. They got my money. I waited in line at Plan 9 Records and spent my nine bucks for the *Decade* tape. That weekend, I took it to a grad-student party as a novelty item, but the hostesses put it on, inflicting it on everyone who showed up. The fact that Duran Duran left "New Moon on Monday" off their greatest hits album made my friends mad, so they pulled their twelve-inch Duran singles from the back of the pile, where they'd been carefully hidden, and slapped the records on. It was a long, sweaty, Duran-filled night.

Listening to it now is like a personally guided tour through my past. Every song is a time capsule full of things that girls want. So I keep listening.

Side 1 starts with "Planet Earth." Duran Duran's first hit. Reached number twelve on the U.K. charts in 1981.

Everybody knows who Duran Duran are, and everybody knows a few of the big hits: "Hungry Like the Wolf," "Rio," "Planet Earth." Some people also know the tiny hits, like "New Moon on Monday" and "Hold Back the Rain." A few of us even made it to Side 2 of the Arcadia record. *So Red the Rose*—now there's a poetic album title.

There are five Durannies, although some periodically leave

the band and get replaced by nobodies. The replacements are never attractive, because the Durannies are too vain to share the stage with anyone as hot as they are.

The Fab Five: Simon Le Bon is the lead singer, the one who wears towels around his neck and had a famous yacht wreck in 1985. He has always claimed Simon Le Bon is his real name. John Taylor is the bassist, and the foxiest member of the group. He did the theme song for the popular film *9½ Weeks*, "I Do What I Do (To Have You)," and starred in the indie film *Sugar Town*. Nick Rhodes is the keyboardist, who is (besides Simon) the only Durannie who has never quit the band. Andy Taylor, the ponytailed guitarist, was the first to quit and go solo. Roger Taylor, the drummer, was the first to quit and not do much of anything.

They first blew into my world in late 1982, when the radio started playing "Hungry Like the Wolf" and "Rio." I knew these songs months before I saw the videos—from the sheer sound, you could tell this was a whole new thing. They claimed they wanted to combine Chic with the Sex Pistols, and talked in lofty art-school terms about their fusion of punk, funk and glam. They wore makeup. They sang mind-humpingly bad poetry, every word of which I loved.

Oh, those fiendish Durannies, with their bat-shit pretensions and their preening pretty-boy bitch faces. Duran Duran, with their ridiculous feverish poetry about the mysterious Cleopatras who seduced and defanged them every few minutes. They made a lot of enemies as well as lifelong fans. Every time they come

255

back and do a reunion tour, the adult women in my life turn into bobby-soxer battalions.

I'm a hard-core Duran Duran fan. I have followed them through side projects and solo albums. I have listened to every single one of their mediocre comeback albums, even the one that was called *Red Carpet Massacre*. I rented the 1986 movie *American Anthem*, a sensitive love story about two Olympic gymnasts, just because Andy Taylor did the pus-gushingly bad theme song.

Hey, I have my moments when I worry about how much I love Duran Duran. I've done things I'm not proud of and frequented chat rooms I won't visit again. I realize they're maybe not the most productive group in the world, or the most talented, or the most proficient. But it doesn't matter. We share secrets, Duran Duran and I. I watched the Live Earth broadcast in 2007 just to see them save the planet. Simon Le Bon told the crowd, "Just coming here is not enough to get what's got to be done, done ... *but* ... if we all sing ... we might just make a stand, right here!"

And what song did Simon choose to save the planet? "Girls on Film." That is why he is Simon, and that is why we love him.

"Girls on Film." Famous for a video with sexy models attacking sumo wrestlers.

Let's not mince words: Duran Duran are famous because girls like them. If a few boys want to come along too, that's fine with Duran Duran, they like the color of our money. But we are the fans they do not care about. They don't need us. They have the girls. They know who keeps them in business.

They've always known this, even in their earliest days. In my collection of DD memorabilia, I treasure their 1981 interview with *Melody Maker*. Nick Rhodes announces, "I've just worked out why so many more blokes are coming to our gigs this time round." Why? "Because they've heard that so many girls come."

In most styles of music, there's a stigma to having this kind of a female audience. When LL Cool J was having his rap battle with Canibus, the deadliest insult Canibus could say was, "Ninety-nine percent of your fans wear high heels." In part, this is just jealousy, but there's also some primal male fear involved. There's the fear that if you have a female audience, male fans won't touch you, and when the females move on to the next cute dude with a catchy song, you will be broke and lonely.

Of course, it goes the other way too. Ladies love LL Cool J—that's what the name stands for, "Ladies Love Cool James"—whereas Canibus never had a hit in the first place. LL's response to the high-heels line? "Ninety-nine percent of your fans don't exist."

"Hungry Like the Wolf." The first time most of us heard Duran Duran, at least in this country. Still the only hit song in history ever to endorse lycanthropic sex.

Simon still sings in the high-pitched yelp of the pop idol. That can be a dangerous thing for a rock singer. It's an old show-biz truism that a low voice has a longer career than a high voice. Even in the old-time radio days, if you were a lightweight tenor, it meant your audience would be female, and that meant you would have a short run. Frank Sinatra became an idol in the 1940s by crooning breathy love ballads to girls while their boyfriends were off fighting World War II. When the soldiers came marching home, Frankie's career crashed—until he made his 1950s comeback with his deep new broken-down-by-love voice. Singers with high voices always try to aim deeper. As baritone Bing Crosby told tenor Dennis Day on *The Jack Benny Program*, "Get your voice down here where the money is, kid."

Simon never worried about any of this. In fact, the mere fact that he decided to go pro with that voice is proof he is made of sterner stuff than people realize.

It can be uncomfortable for a boy to watch the frenzied, uninhibited enthusiasm of girl fans screaming for their idols, whether it's Sinatra, the Beatles or Michael Jackson. That is partly jealousy too—who wouldn't want to be the one who inspires girls to make that kind of noise? But it's also partly because we envy that enthusiasm. The archetypal girl fan does not have to worry about whether music is cool or valid or authentic. If it makes her dance or gets her hot, she screams.

Boys do not scream, so we get threatened by all this libidinal energy. As the musical philosopher Lil' Kim has noted, inside every man is a *baaaad* girl. And that bad girl can scare the bejeezus out of us. The lady makes demands.

There's a story I love about the Beatles' manager, Brian Epstein, a gay man who could never publicly acknowledge the intensity of his love for this band he'd discovered. One night, on tour in America, he gave himself a special treat he'd never indulged before. He sneaked into the back of the crowd, anonymous in the dark, stood with the girls, and screamed as loud as he'd always wanted to.

When I hear Duran Duran, part of me wants to scream for them and part of me wants to be the guy who the girls are screaming for. I guess that's why they keep me feeling fascination. Duran Duran are a girls' band who have stayed famous by being true to their girls; they do not let this stigma get to them. They are flamboyantly pleased to be adored by females. They do not get rattled by the screams.

Next up on the hit parade is "Rio." The title track to their second and biggest album. Still their most famous video, with their second-most-laughed-at lyric: "It means so much to me, like a birthday or a pretty view." Gloriously terrible sax solo too.

They cared nothing for rock standards of authenticity. They had three guys in the band named Taylor, as in clothes-makers, and I didn't know what was more brilliant, the fact that it was their real name or the fact that they weren't related. They came from Birmingham, and if I'd known anything about Great Britain, I would have known it was a grim industrial steel town where the urge to break out of gender confines must have been overpowering. But I didn't. All I knew was the way they draped themselves on the inner sleeve of *Rio*. For a few months, it was hard to tell Nick from John, unless John was sporting his bare-chest-under-white-blazer-and-one-of-La-Toya-Jackson's-spare-headbands look.

I still get that frisson every time I see the "Rio" video. Simon's on his yacht, wearing some kind of powder-blue mesh tank top.

A girl swims through the ocean carrying a pink phone, which Simon answers so he can sing the second verse to another girl on another boat. I love the girl who strolls out of the surf with a knife strapped to her thigh. (Why, Lord, why? Why didn't that look catch on?) I love the girl who stretches on the love seat and yawns indulgently while John nervously fumbles with the champagne.

I have no idea how many different girls are in this video, but they're all Rio to me, and I fell in love with all of her. The way she winks at the end, as if she has been here before. Duran Duran are not the first rock-and-roll sailor boys to zoom through her harbor, and they won't be the last. She is older than the sand upon which she dances. You will pass away, lover boy, just another pair of dancing footprints in the sand, but Rio will roll on. Creamed jeans are made of this!

Side 2 starts with "The Reflex." Their first and biggest U.S. number-one hit, even though everybody likes "Rio" a lot better. The lead singer of the Fixx denounced this song, saying, "There's a soul flapping in the breeze there."

Boys were threatened by Duran Duran, which was understandable. They were the first popular band to get dismissed as a video band, an MTV scam that gullible girls got brainwashed into liking. John Lydon of Public Image Ltd., formerly Johnny Rotten, sneered, "As for you poor little cows who buy Duran Duran records, you need serious help 'cause these people are conning you."

That was a popular sentiment. When the Clash called their 1985 album *Cut the Crap*, Duran Duran was probably the crap they meant. Sweatband-wearing rock prudes Dire Straits rustled up a huge hit called "Money for Nothing," raging against them. "That little faggot with the earring and the makeup / Yeah buddy, that's his own hair." Dire Straits didn't wear earrings, makeup or hair for that matter. They just wore sweatbands.

Boys around the world were arguing with their girlfriends, trying to explain why Duran Duran were a fraud, a smoke-and-mirrors show, an imperialist plot, a joke. They probably didn't write their own songs or play their own instruments; they were a soulless corporate product. If I'd had a girlfriend, I probably would have given her the same argument. Maybe I liked Duran Duran so much because I could console myself for not having a girlfriend. By being a DD fan, I was part of the problem that was making so many other boys so mad.

Lots of bands complained that Duran Duran and the other new-wave hair-hoppers were taking up valuable airtime that rightfully belonged to the American bands turning up the soil of the punk underground: the Minutemen, the Flesh Eaters, D.O.A., Big Boys or Black Flag. Some of my favorite bands grappled with the moral ambiguities of the whole DD phenemonon: X came out against them ("I Must Not Think Bad Thoughts"), while the Replacements found them amusing ("Androgynous"). These were both great songs. Not as great as "Hungry Like the Wolf," though.

"Is There Something I Should Know?" This ballad has Duran Duran's most famous line: "You're about as easy as a nuclear war." No, I don't know what it means.

The first time I met Duran Duran, they were called Shaun Cassidy.

Maureen Connelly brought the Shaun Cassidy album into school one day, in that fateful spring of 1977. The entire girl half of the fourth grade sat rapt as Shaun whispered his secret girl code: "Da Doo Ron Ron." Da doo ron ron? What the hell did that mean? The dewy look on every female face in the room made me eager to know more, but Shaun wasn't telling. Da doo ron ron.

All of us boys hated Shaun Cassidy, feared him, made fun of him, boycotted his *Hardy Boys* television show. We were singing "fuck you ron ron ron, fuck you ron ron" to his *Dynamite* cover shot, cursing his blond perfection and his three-foot-wide blue eyes; I rejoiced when *Mad* magazine renamed him "Shorn Chastity." What we didn't realize was that Shaun didn't understand this girl language any better than we did. We had no idea "Da Doo Ron Ron" was an old '60s girl-group song by the Crystals. Shaun didn't know what "da doo ron ron" meant either.

A few months later, the same damn thing happened all over again. Except now it was Melissa Kaiser bringing the album into class, and Shaun's name was now Andy Gibb. He was even blonder and cuter, with ringlets that cascaded down his head like the wool of a sacrificial lamb. That's when it dawned on me that this cycle would never end. By the time Andy Gibb was up to his third or fourth hit, there would be another one, and then another. Only the names would change, and even then not much. It was like *Showgirls*: there's always someone younger and hungrier coming up behind you on the stairs.

This proved to be correct. Every few months there was always someone new, except now my sisters were old enough to command the radio and buy records, so I heard them at home rather than just at school. They kept coming, the Rick Springfields and John Stamoses (Stami?) and Loverboys and REO Speedwagons. And—just in time for high school—Duran Duran, a new breed of boys on film.

The average girlie-idol pop star has a short run, partly because girls are fickle, but mostly because boys always want to be taken seriously. So they try going rock, and get alpha bravo'd by reality, at which point the girls have found someone else. Your average pop star gets famous by acting girlie—and as soon as he gets to the top, he frantically tries to get rid of the girls and starts trying to get taken seriously by the boys. Hell, even Shaun Cassidy tried to go boy-rock eventually, doing an album of Who and Talking Heads covers produced by Todd Rundgren.

It's the oldest story in the book, but the stars never learn. They wash off the makeup, grow some stubble, start frowning and crossing their arms in the band photos. Hey, is that a brick wall? Let's stand in front of it! It never, *never* works.

Okay, right, it worked for George Michael. And Justin Timberlake, and I guess you could count Bon Jovi too, although I'd trade their entire mature classic-rock phase for one chorus of "Livin' on a Prayer." But look at the wreckage. Poor Ricky Nelson—he changed his name to Rick, disavowed his teenage-idol past, started playing sensitive hippie country rock. The Bay City Rollers became the Rollers and started writing adult rock songs about how lonely it was being teen idols on the road. The New

Kids on the Block changed their name to NKOTB and tried to win the serious hip-hop crowd with "No More Games." Frankie Goes to Hollywood claimed, "We're not a girl's band. We're a man's band." (Well, that was understandable.) Spandau Ballet went metal. Milli Vanilli tried singing.

Even Poison, those frou-frou bubble-metal skanks—they scrubbed off the Max Factor, got serious, did an acoustic ballad called "Stand." "You got to stand for what you believe." Wait, I'm getting advice from Bret Michaels? About standing for what I believe? I'll tell you what I believe, Bret. I believe in "Talk Dirty to Me," and C.C. DeVille, and Rikki Rockett, especially on the album where you were credited with "Vocalizin' and Socializin'" while C.C. was "Sticks, Tricks, and Lipstick Fix." I believe in every single episode of *Rock of Love*, especially the one where the crazed stripper steals the gym socks from the roller rink. But "Stand"? Nay, Bret—this is not what I believe in, and you never believed it either, which is why I believe in you. Hug?

Every star is afraid of the scent of Bubble Yum, the snap of barrettes. But can you blame them? It's got to be unnerving being up there in the girlie lights, hearing the screams of the lust-crazed bacchantes. It scared the ancient Greeks—Orpheus, the inventor of song, was ripped to pieces by lovesick sea nymphs because his voice was *just too hot*. Euripides wrote *The Bacchae*, about the dancing ladies who worship Dionysus and get driven so mad by his music that they rip off their husbands' heads.

If Simon Le Bon ever feels it's a drag to get up there every night and remember the plot to "The Chauffeur" and act surprised every goddamn time Rio shows up to run him down ("Wooo! Hey now! Look at that!"), he keeps it locked inside his pretty little head. If he owns any sensible shoes, he never gets caught wearing them in public. If any of the Durannies have any fits of male pride where they feel it's demeaning to tart themselves up for the ladies, they keep it to themselves. These men let their self-doubt float across their sky like a fluffy black cloud. Once, when an interviewer asked who would play them in a movie, John Taylor named some guy from *Dynasty*, Simon picked Eddie Murphy and Nick Rhodes said, "Joan Crawford, just because she wore great shoulder pads." Now *that's* a star talking.

"A View to a Kill." Their second U.S. number-one hit. The theme to a James Bond movie that nobody has ever seen. The video has John Taylor shooting a bunch of people on the Eiffel Tower.

When I was writing for the MTV Video Music Awards, in the summer of 2003, I wrote a speech about them. Kelly Osbourne and Avril Lavigne were giving the band a Lifetime Achievement Award, and I wrote their speech. They are both huge DD fans, even though they weren't born until 1984, circa "The Wild Boys." It was a daunting task. How could I do justice to the subject—not to the band, who I'd written about a million times, but to the fans. Could I do justice to the girls who were screaming for this band before Kelly or Avril showed up to scream along?

It was a surprise award for the band. They thought they were merely invited to appear onstage and present an award to somebody else; Kelly Osbourne and Avril Lavigne came out with the trophy and sprung it on Duran Duran as a surprise. The band looked pleased—but not humbled. Who wants to seem them humbled?

Kelly and Avril delivered the speech beautifully, passionately. Kelly sounded like a preacher, getting religion, waving her hands in the air and getting the crowd screaming. Every time she yelled out another DD song title, the screams got louder. She was on fire. I was watching from my seat in the back of Radio City Music Hall, where I was just another dude. But Kelly Osbourne and Avril Lavigne—they were girls who loved Duran Duran.

"Notorious." A huge hit in 1986, produced by Nile Rodgers of Chic. This was the first DD hit without Roger and Andy. It was also the first hit that made people say, "Oooo, I like this one. Who is it? Duran Duran? What the hell are they doing still around?"

There's a character in a Shakespeare play who describes life as "six or seven winters more," but what she really meant was "six or seven Duran Duran records more." They always keep making more. More than you would guess without having to look it up. No matter how big a fan you are, you probably haven't flipped through Nick Rhodes's photographic collection *Interference,* or listened to Simon's solo version of "Ordinary World" with Luciano Pavarotti. Duran Duran have more records than you've heard, more than they remember, more than anyone wants. They've stuck around so long, they have aged into the despot dowagers of new wave. To tell the truth, even a hard-core fan has to be stunned by their staying power.

In the '90s, they had an urban radio smash with their cover of Grandmaster Flash's "White Lines (Don't Do It)." But they don't really worry about hits anymore. Now they make records with Justin Timberlake and Timbaland, just to prove they can. They seem to be constantly doing reunion tours. Once in a while, you catch them taking themselves seriously, and although those moments are brief, they're reassuring and kind of poignant. There's a VH1 *Classic Albums* documentary on the making of *Rio*. It's downright sweet to see Nick Rhodes in the studio at the mixing board, turning up the guitar track from the master tapes of "Rio." "It's a hell of a guitar sound, actually," Nick muses. "Andy always used to use Marshalls but then he was quite experimental with his pedals at that time too, so I'm sure it was chorused and flanged and delayed a little." John Taylor adds, "He had a lot of knowledge of the fretboard." Oh, puh-fucking-lease! What are we, Jeff Beck now? This is a Duran Duran record!

I feel I still have so much to learn from Duran Duran. They're like the musical version of the sensei that Uma Thurman goes to study martial arts with in *Kill Bill*. They are my new-wave senseis. What do we expect from DD? Egomania. Ridiculousness. Sexual hysteria. A little humor if we're lucky. You will never meet anybody in your life who has ever felt disappointed by them or anything they do. But somehow, that just makes it safer to love them.

Does anybody know or care what DD themselves want? Does anybody worry that they are not finding artistic fulfillment? Does anyone wonder what they are "really like" or how they "really feel" in everyday life? Maybe Simon likes to slip into a terry-cloth robe and read romance novels in the tub. Maybe John roots for the Pittsburgh Penguins. Maybe Nick sneaks into the basement and picks up an acoustic guitar to play Bob Dylan songs. Who cares? Nobody. Not even me.

In general, girls do not really care what goes on in Simon's brain. They don't want him sincere or confessional. I love the tender ballad "Save a Prayer," so whenever it comes on the car radio, I turn it up. But my wife, Ally, just snickers, "Sensitive DD!" Girls do not like "Save a Prayer" as much as they like "Hungry Like the Wolf." They do not want a Simon who feels adult emotions; they want him to ooze vanity and lechery. So "Save a Prayer" is now an obscure deep cut, while "Hungry Like the Wolf" is a song known to every human being on planet Earth.

Why? Don't ask me. I love "Save a Prayer." I'm a boy.

"All She Wants Is." A Top 40 hit in 1989. It's traditional for a band to conclude their greatest-hits album by sticking on some crap new song, as a way of saying "we're still working" or "we do weddings, parties, anything." But Duran Duran didn't have room to do this, because they were still scoring hits. And they weren't finished yet.

Ally is the girl I love, so she is the girl I talk to about Duran Duran. When we are out dancing at our favorite sleazy rock bar and "Rio" comes on, as it always does, she and I are the "two of a billion stars" Simon is singing about. We make sure to lock eyes when that line comes around and sing it to each other. Since Ally's an astrophysicist, she knows all about stars and quasars and tidal debris and accreted satellite material. Her universe is such a big place, full of so many galaxies—100 billion of them, with 100 billion stars apiece, which means 10 to the 22nd power stars—that it's terrifying to think of the odds that we found each other. We want to freeze the perfect moment, hold on to it, at least long enough to understand it. But it dances on with us or without us, so we jump in and try to keep up. The universe is expanding, and we are just two of a billion stars.

For Catholics, the decade is part of the rosary. There are five decades in a rosary, ten Hail Marys in a decade, each devoted to a mystery—the Joyful Mysteries, the Sorrowful Mysteries, the Glorious Mysteries. It goes around in a loop. So "All She Wants Is" brings us back around to where the decade started: a girl and what she wants. That's where the mystery begins.

Acknowledgments

Thanks to everybody who has helped me. My genius editor Carrie Thornton has provided the spirit of Depeche Mode. My genius agent Daniel Greenberg has provided the spirit of Run-DMC. I am savagely grateful to all my friends, some of whom might find their voices or stories mangled by memory in this book. Names have been changed, either to protect privacy or because the radio was on and I wasn't really paying attention while you were talking. Cheers to those who remember things differently—as Paul Westerberg would say, your guess is more or less as bad as mine.

All love to my family, especially my mom and dad—Bob and Mary Sheffield—for teaching me about love and music and everything else. My sisters are my heroes: the inspirational Ann

Sheffield, the dynamic Tracey Mackey, the extraordinary Caroline Hanlon. When Tracey read the Hall & Oates chapter, she wrote me: "You STILL got the Private Eyes clapping wrong! It's clap, THEN clap-clap. You are such a boy!" So it's official: I still can't clap to "Private Eyes." But bless my sisters for getting me this close.

Thanks to my sisters' flawless taste in men, I have two brothers, Bryant Mackey and John Hanlon, and over the past ten years we have met eight of the planet's all-time coolest people: Charlie, Sarah, Allison, David, Sydney, Jackie, Mallory and Maggie. Since a couple of these people plan to marry Taylor Swift when they grow up, let me thank Taylor in advance. Huge love to Donna, Joe, Sean and Jake Needham; Tony and Shirley Viera; Jonathan, Karianne, Ashley and Amber Polak, most of whom can beat me at Wii Just Dance.

Thank you to all the amazing people at Dutton, especially Brian Tart, Lily Kosner, Christine Ball, Carrie Swetonic, Julia Gilroy, Amanda Walker and Tala Oszkay. Gregg Kulick, who designed the cover of this book as well as *Love Is a Mix Tape*, is a brilliant man of vision, as you can see for yourself. Crazy snaps to Jay Sones, Maria Elias and Monika Verma.

Thanks to everyone at *Rolling Stone*, especially the mighty Will Dana, who provided invaluable editorial illumination and taught me to appreciate Side 2 of *Tattoo You*, Sean Woods, Caryn Ganz, Alison Weinflash, Nathan Brackett, Jason Fine, Kevin O'Donnell, Tom Walsh, Nicole Frehsee, Jonathan Ringen, Brian Hiatt, Christian Hoard, Michael Endelman, Coco McPherson,

Erica Futterman, John Dioso, David Fricke and Andy Greene, with a special tip of the cap and a "Machine Gun" air-guitar solo to Jann Wenner.

To paraphrase Oran "Juice" Jones, me without my friends would be like cornflakes without the milk. Gavin Edwards taped me Prince's *Sign O' the Times* in 1987 and provided beyond-valiant editorial help. Joe Levy played me R.E.M.'s Out of Time over the phone in 1991 and brought the noise as an editorial samurai lord. These two have been music gurus and blood brothers to me since the '80s. I am always grateful to Chuck Klosterman, who pointed out that I invariably blather about Paul McCartney after the third beer. Sean Howe forced me to reappraise the Level 42 legacy. Jenny Eliscu makes everything louder.

For various forms of assistance with this book, including but not limited to the correct spelling of "hypotenuse," I bow to Darcey Steinke, Melissa Maerz, Joe Gross, Marc Spitz, Melissa Eltringham, Lizzy Goodman, Sasha Frere-Jones, Alex Pappademas, Marc Weidenbaum, Jen Sudul Edwards, Jeffrey Stock, Jennie Boddy, Niki Kanodia, Nils Bernstein, Phoebe Reilly, Flynn Monks, Asif Ahmed, Tyler Magill, Ivan Kreilkamp, Elizabeth Webster, Lisa Miller, Isabelle George Rosett, Jessica Hopper, Karl Precoda, Nancy Whang, Donata Dabrowska, Robert Christgau, Alfred Soto, Greil Marcus, Dave Rimmer, John Leland, Tom Nawrocki, Tracey Pepper, Heather Rosett, Maureen Callahan, Maria Falgoust, Sarah Wilson and WTJU. Barak Rosenbloom got me living high in the dirty business of ice cream. Thanks to everybody at Enid's, where most of this book was written, and the Hold Steady, who I was usually listening to. Thanks to whoever typed in the lyrics to Def Leppard's "Photograph" on the Sing Sing karaoke machine because you give me the joy of hearing Fred and Melissa debate whether it's "down to the rock-and-roll clown" or "bow to the rock-and-roll crown." (Still arguing about Def Leppard after fifteen years of marriage! An inspiration to us all.) Thanks to the musicians in this book, too. They all deserve big, wet sloppy kisses, except I just flossed.

Most of all, eternal love and gratitude to my lovecat bride, Ally, for her inspiration, her support and making sure that whenever Ashford & Simpson come on the speakers while we're waiting in line at the airport, I will get to sing along with her. Solid as a rock.